QUILTING
THE NATIONAL PARKS

For Mandy, who started it all,
and Kyle, for being by my side every step of the way.

QUILTING
THE NATIONAL PARKS

20 Original Designs Inspired by
the Beauty of Our National Parks

Stephanie Forster

weldon**owen**

CONTENTS

THROWS

BED QUILTS

RESOURCES 203

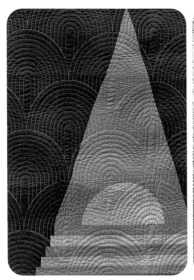  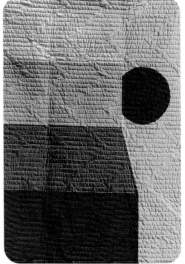

INTRODUCTION

The United States National Parks are some of the greatest travel destinations in the country for families and adventure-seekers alike. Home to incredible wildlife and activities such as hiking, rock climbing, kayaking, snowshoeing, and snorkeling, these historic lands truly offer something for everyone to discover. With more than 84 million acres of land, the National Parks preserve ecosystems and protect endangered plant and animal species. Besides conserving our environment, these parks also have a positive impact on our well-being. Being outside and connected to nature is known to decrease stress and anxiety, increase problem solving, and promote creativity.

With this book you can celebrate the natural beauty of the world we live in by bringing these scenic parks and stunning landscapes into your home. These quilt patterns, inspired by twenty of the sixty-three National Parks, come in five different project sizes, including pillow, wall hanging, baby, throw, and bed quilts. These projects reflect the diverse terrains of our National Parks, from the rugged mountains in Hawaii to the glaciers in Alaska, the shorelines of Lake Michigan to the deep-sea depths of the Gulf of Mexico, and the desert climates of California to the northern lights in Minnesota.

For new quilters, Yellowstone is a great introduction project to learn the basics of piecing simple shapes together. To grow your skills and learn how to sew curves and make half-rectangle triangles and half-square triangles, Zion incorporates all three of these blocks in a simple pattern. Intermediate quilters will enjoy the more intricate designs of Congaree, Joshua Tree, and Olympic National Parks. As you progress through these projects, you will learn about the history and unique features of each park, as well as the inspiration behind each design.

Just like the protected lands of the National Parks that will be preserved and enjoyed for generations to come, your quilts will be passed down and cherished from generation to generation, memorializing not only the picturesque landscapes of each park but also the love and creativity you dedicated to each quilt. I hope when you adventure out to a National Park (or all sixty-three!), you not only capture the spectacular scenery while taking iconic Quilts in the Wild photos, but that you also find peace and your own inspiration in nature.

The Basics

TOOLS

Here is a quick list of the must-haves for every quilting project.

CURVED QUILTING SAFETY PINS OR SPRAY BASTE Used to keep the quilt layers (quilt top, batting, and backing) together, pins are a great reusable option and my preference for basting quilts. Spray basting is a quick and easy method to sandwich all of the quilt layers together, though it can be messy and is not as environmentally friendly as reusable pins.

DRY ERASE MARKER Useful for marking rulers when trimming half-rectangle triangles (HRTs).

FABRIC MARKING TOOL This is most often a water-soluble marker or a hera marker used to mark quilting lines.

FABRIC SCISSORS Useful for cutting batting, snipping threads, and trimming various fabrics. I keep my scissors within reach of my sewing machine for easy use.

HAND QUILTING NEEDLE Used to hand quilt or attach binding to the back of your quilt.

IRON Used to press fabric and seams. I used a basic iron for many years before upgrading. My favorite feature of my new iron is the auto-shutoff feature, which has alleviated many "Did I turn my iron off?" fears.

IRONING SURFACE An ironing board or a flat surface to place a wool pressing mat.

PAINTER'S TAPE Used to tape backing to the floor when basting your quilt.

PINS Used to pin fabric together during piecing; pins help keep everything aligned and in place.

QUILTING GLOVES Specialty gloves with grippers to better guide your quilt through your machine. Gardening gloves are a great substitute.

QUILTING RULERS Used to make accurate and straight fabric cuts. My most frequently used ruler is my 6 in. x 24 in. (15.2 cm x 61 cm) ruler. Other ruler recommendations include a 4 in. x 36 in. (10.2 cm x 91.4 cm) ruler for extra-long cuts or trimming large blocks, a 15 in. x 15 in. (38 cm x 38 cm) square ruler for squaring up quilts and trimming blocks, and a 6 in. x 6 in. (15.2 cm x 15.2 cm) square ruler for trimming small blocks and smaller subcuts.

ROTARY CUTTERS Used to cut fabric using a sharp, wheeled blade. Cutter blades come in a variety of sizes: a 45 mm blade is common for cutting most fabric, while an 18 mm blade is useful for cutting around templates.

SEAM RIPPER A small tool used to cut and remove stitches.

SELF-HEALING CUTTING MAT Used to cut fabric using a rotary cutter, they protect your cutting surface and come in various sizes. If you have the space for it, I recommend using a 24 in. x 36 in. (61 cm x 91.4 cm) cutting mat.

SEWING MACHINE A basic sewing machine is all you need to get started on your quilting journey. I bought a basic starter sewing machine and used it consistently for more than ten years before finally upgrading.

SEWING MACHINE NEEDLES Used in your sewing machine; refer to your machine's manual to determine the best needle to use.

STARCH Used to stiffen fabric, it's sprayed on and then pressed to make fabric easier to work with when cutting and sewing.

THIMBLE Used to protect your fingers when hand quilting.

THREAD For piecing and quilting, a 50-weight cotton thread is recommended. For hand quilting, an 8-weight cotton thread is recommended.

WALKING FOOT Used for machine quilting, a walking foot evenly guides the layers of your quilt through your machine to create even stitches.

THE FABRIC

CHOOSING THE FABRIC

The first step in the quilting process—and the most exciting for me—is choosing the fabric for my quilt. I frequently use my Art Gallery Fabrics color cards, which are swatches of their *Pure Solids* line—my go-to and favorite solid-color fabrics. Art Gallery Fabrics have a silky-smooth texture, and the colors are incredibly rich and vibrant. For this book I used Art Gallery Fabrics *Pure Solids* exclusively. There are more than 150 colors in their *Pure Solids* line, so if you want to switch up your National Park scenery, grab your color cards and start experimenting!

PREPARING THE FABRIC

You've chosen your fabric and you're ready to start, but first, the age-old question: "To prewash or not to prewash?" Prewashing your fabric can prevent fabric bleeding and shrinkage and remove chemicals. If you want to avoid the quilt crinkle that happens after washing your finished piece, prewashing the fabric might be the right choice for you. If you love the look of a freshly laundered, crinkly quilt, skip the prewash. Unless you are extra sensitive, you may not want to prewash because some of the chemicals used in fabric factories can help stabilize the fabric and prevent wrinkles. If you're worried about bleeding, throw a color-catching sheet in the washing machine with your quilt. If I'm using a fabric that has an extra-inky smell to it, I might throw it in the wash before using it, but usually I skip the prewash.

STARCHING AND PRESSING THE FABRIC

Once your fabric is prewashed (or not), it's time to starch and press. Starching your fabric increases its stiffness and rigidity, making it easier to work with as you press, cut, and sew. I use Mary Ellen's Best Press starch on my fabric as I press. Whether or not you decide to use starch, do not skip the pressing step. Pressing helps remove wrinkles from your fabric and ensures that your cuts are more accurate. Set your iron to the cotton setting and press each fabric for your quilt.

CUTTING THE FABRIC

A few pointers about cutting your fabric:

- Standing while cutting is the most effective cutting method so you can use your body weight on both the rotary cutter and the ruler to prevent slippage.

- Double-check your cutting instructions before making the final cut to ensure your ruler is placed accurately.

- Align the fold of the width of fabric (WOF) on the grid of your cutting mat, then line up your ruler with the gridlines and trim off any uneven fabric edges.

- Cut away from your body and make sure that your rotary blade is sharp, so you are making efficient cuts.

- Label each piece as you go and keep your cut pieces in numerical order, grouped by fabric. (Most pieces are used in succession when piecing together a project.)

- Cutting instructions do not take directional fabric into account; you may need additional fabric if you are not using a solid fabric.

- The New River Gorge National Park wall hanging has several cuts per WOF; see Figure 1 for cutting diagrams. The Dry Tortugas National Park quilt has large template cuts per WOF; see Figure 2 for cutting diagrams. Note: A and B on the diagrams refer to the templates, while fabric letter is referenced to the left of each WOF.

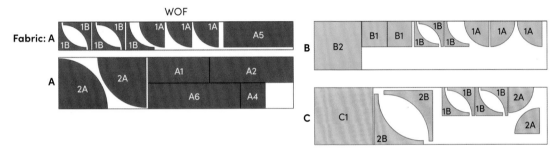

Figure 1

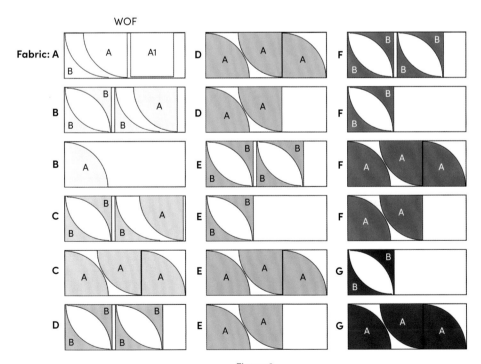

Figure 2

CUTTING AND ASSEMBLING BLOCKS

The patterns in this book use four different types of blocks: half- and quarter-curve blocks, half-rectangle triangles (HRTs), and half-square triangles (HSTs). If you are new to any of these blocks, I recommend practicing with scrap fabric before starting your project, especially for curves and HRTs. This section provides detailed information on cutting, piecing, and trimming each of these blocks. Refer to each pattern individually for trimming sizes. Note: Some projects will have unused HRT units remaining after piecing.

CUTTING BLOCKS

Half-Curves

1 To cut half-curve templates, fold WOF to the width of Template A, place Template A on WOF, and cut, as shown in Figure 1. Repeat, refolding fabric for all subsequent cuts. To cut Template B, fold WOF to the width of Template B, place Template B on WOF, and cut. Repeat, refolding fabric for all subsequent cuts.

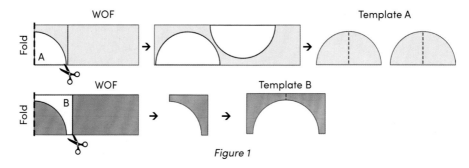

Figure 1

2 Pair each Template B piece with its corresponding Template A piece (Template 1A pairs with Template 1B, and Template 2A pairs with Template 2B, etc.). Fold each piece in half and mark the center with a crease. Lay Template B on top of Template A, right sides together, as shown in Figure 2. Line up the creased center lines, then pin at the center point. Pin as often as desired, then sew a .25 in. (.6 cm) seam around the curve very slowly, carefully adjusting your fabric as needed. Press the seam. Repeat for each template pair. These are now called Template Blocks.

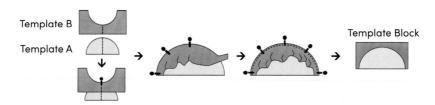

Figure 2

3 Refer to the specific pattern you're working to determine trim size. Fold each Template Block in half again to mark the center of your block with a crease. Trim the bottom of the Template Block (the side with the curve) first, trimming only enough excess fabric to create a flat edge, then trim the top. To trim the length, keep your creased line centered and trim each side equally, as shown in Figure 3.

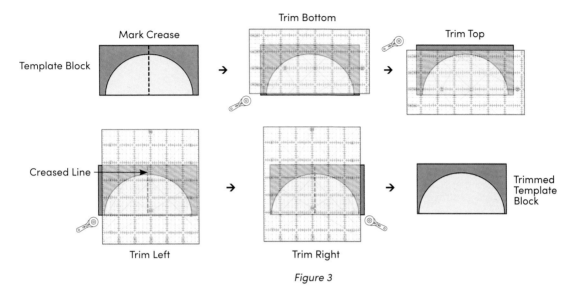

Figure 3

Quarter-Curves

1 To cut quarter-curve template pieces, place Template A and B on WOF and cut, as shown in Figure 1. Rotate the templates to yield more cuts from WOF.

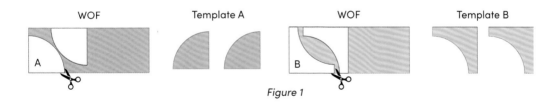

Figure 1

2 Pair each Template B piece with its corresponding Template A piece (Template 1A pairs with Template 1B, and Template 2A pairs with Template 2B, etc.). Fold each piece in half and mark the center with a crease. Lay Template B on top of Template A, right sides together, as shown in Figure 2. Line up the creased center lines, then pin at the center point. Pin as often as desired, then sew a scant .25 in. (.6 cm) seam around the curve very slowly, carefully adjusting your fabric as needed. Press the seam. These are now called Template Blocks.

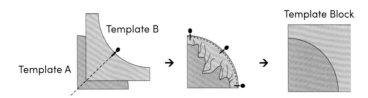

Figure 2

3 Refer to the specific pattern you're working to determine trim size. To trim quarter-curve blocks, trim excess fabric from the curved edges first, then trim the remainder of the block to the width indicated for each pattern. Pay attention to the Template B fabric to ensure each side is trimmed equally, leaving a .25 in. (.6 cm) seam allowance, as shown in Figure 3.

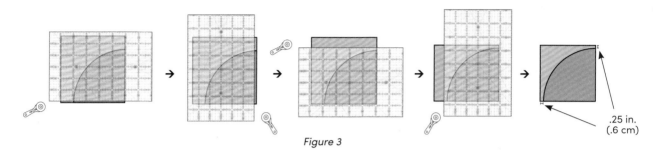

Figure 3

4 Yosemite National Park quilt Template Block 2: Trim excess fabric from the curved edges first, then trim the remainder of the block to 7 in. x 3 in. (17.8 cm x 7.6 cm). Pay attention to the Template B fabric to ensure each side is trimmed equally, leaving a .25 in. (.6 cm) seam allowance, as shown in Figure 4. Template Block 2 was sized up to account for extra trimming space.

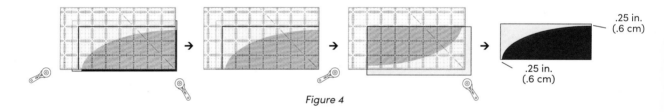

Figure 4

Half-Rectangle Triangles (HRTs)

1 HRTs are sewn in two different orientations (right and left). Refer to each pattern to determine the required amount for each right/left orientation. To sew each HRT, pair each cut triangle with its corresponding cut triangle, as shown in Figure 1 (ex. A1 + B1). Line up each A1/B1 pair and place the right sides together, overlapping the triangles with a .25 in. (.6 cm) corner on each side. Pin and sew a .25 in. (.6 cm) seam along the edge. Refer to each pattern to determine the required amount and fabric combinations of HRTs.

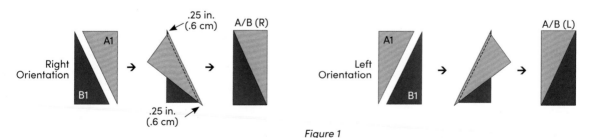

Figure 1

2 HRTs are trimmed without perfect corners (a mitered corner with a 45-degree angle and sharp point) due to the rectangle's oblong shape. Figure 2 shows how each HRT will look after it is trimmed. Prior to trimming, find the .25 in. (.6 cm) Seam Allowance Square within each corner of the Trim Size (see each pattern). Each .25 in. (.6 cm) mark indicates where the seams will match when piecing.

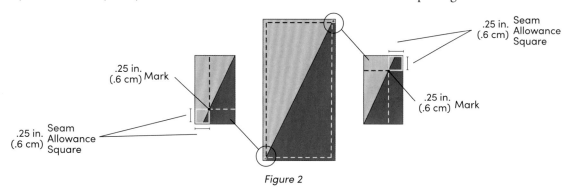

Figure 2

3 To trim HRTs, first mark the Trim Size (Figures 3 and 4 use 2.75 in. x 5 in. [7 cm x 12.7 cm] as an example) on your ruler with a dry erase marker or tape. Next, find the .25 in. (.6 cm) Seam Allowance Square in each corner and mark each .25 in. (.6 cm) Mark location on your ruler using a dry erase marker. For this example, Right Orientation HRT .25 in. (.6 cm) Marks are found in the Top Left (at 2.5 in. x .25 in. [6.3 cm x .6 cm]) and Bottom Right (at .25 in. x 4.75 in. [.6 cm x 12 cm]), and Left Orientation HRT .25 in. (.6 cm) Marks are found in the Top Right (at .25 in. x .25 in. [.6 cm x .6 cm]) and Bottom Left (at 2.5 in. x 4.75 in. [.6 cm x 12 cm]). The width is measured from the right side of the unit and the length is measured from the top of the unit. Patterns with long and thin HRTs (such as Zion and Yosemite) follow the same trimming steps, with the HRT rotated at an angle beneath your ruler, as shown in Figure 5.

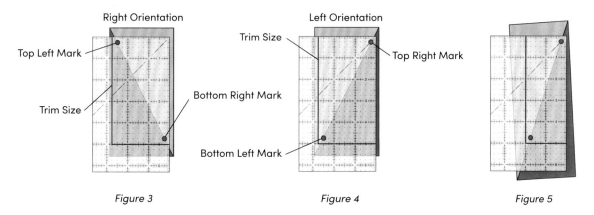

Figure 3   *Figure 4*   *Figure 5*

4 After finding the .25 in. (.6 cm) Marks within the .25 in. (.6 cm) Seam Allowance Squares, use the diagonal seam on the HRT to intersect the .25 in. (.6 cm) Marks in each corner. Next, trim the right and top of the HRT, as shown in Figure 6. Figure 7 shows the trimmed right side and top of a Left Orientation HRT with the .25 in. (.6 cm) Seam Allowance Square.

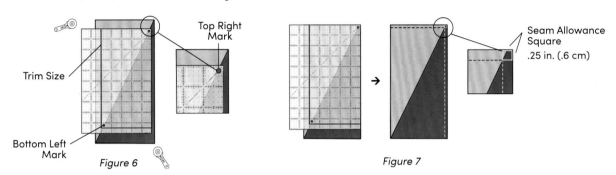

Figure 6

Figure 7

5 Rotate the HRT 180 degrees and align the left and bottom of your trimmed HRT with the marked Trim Size lines on your ruler, as shown in Figure 8. Intersect the .25 in. (.6 cm) Marks along the HRT seam and trim the right and top of the HRT. To trim Right Orientation HRTs, find the .25 in. (.6 cm) Seam Allowance Square and .25 in. (.6 cm) Marks on the opposite side of the ruler within each Trim Size.

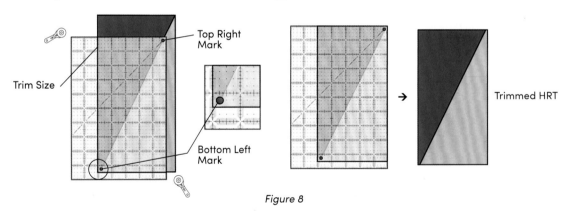

Figure 8

6 To trim HRT 3, find the .25 in. (.6 cm) Marks in the Bottom Left and Right, and the Top Right (or Left, depending on HRT orientation), as shown in Figure 9. Intersect all three seam lines with .25 in. (.6 cm) Marks, and trim the right and top of the HRT. Rotate your HRT 180 degrees and align the left and bottom of your trimmed HRT with the marked Trim Size lines on your ruler, as shown in Figure 10. Find the .25 in. (.6 cm) Marks in the Top Left and Right, and the Bottom Left (or Right, depending on HRT orientation). Intersect all three seam lines with .25 in. (.6 cm) Marks, and trim the right and top of the HRT.

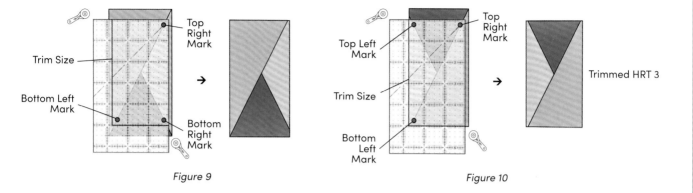

Figure 9   Figure 10

Half-Square Triangles (HSTs)

1 To make two-at-a-time HSTs, pair each square right sides together and mark a line on the diagonal of each square, as shown in Figure 1. Sew a .25 in. (.6 cm) seam on each side of the marked center line. Cut in half on the marked diagonal line and press the seams open. Each set of paired squares will make two HSTs.

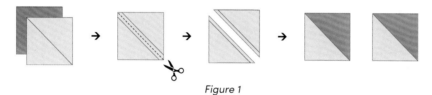

Figure 1

2 To trim HSTs, first find the Trim Size on your ruler to visualize where you will trim. Align the diagonal seam of your HST with the 45-degree line on your ruler. Next, trim the right and top of your HST. Rotate your HST 180 degrees and align the left and bottom of your trimmed HST with the Trim Size lines on your ruler, as shown in Figure 2. Trim the remaining sides of your HST.

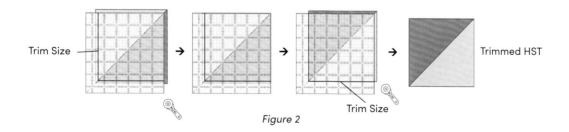

Figure 2

ASSEMBLING ("PIECING") YOUR BLOCKS

Follow the piecing instructions for each project, using a .25 in. (.6 cm) seam allowance (unless specifically stated to use a scant seam allowance). To save time, chain piece (see p. 206) your HRTs and HSTs. See Figures 1–6 for examples of written instructions and diagrams when piecing with curves, HSTs, and HRTs.

Piecing with Curves

Piecing instructions for Template Blocks are listed as B/C or C/B, with the first letter referring to the fabric name in the Template A position. Refer to Figure 1 for half- and quarter-curve Template A and B placement. See Figures 2–4 for an example of Template Block written instructions and how diagrams are displayed in this book.

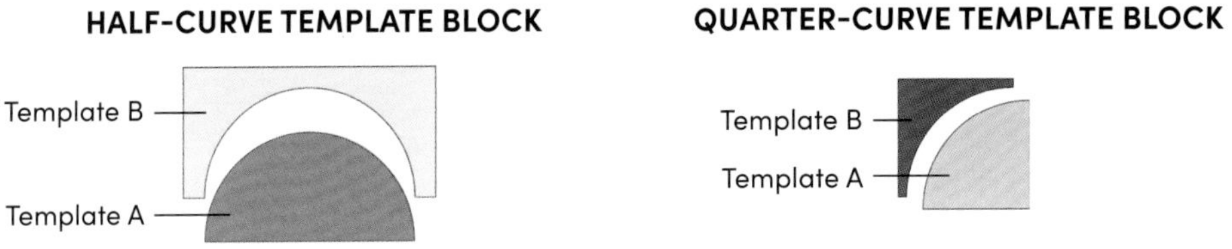

HALF-CURVE TEMPLATE BLOCK   QUARTER-CURVE TEMPLATE BLOCK

Template B

Template A

Template B

Template A

Figure 1

Figures 2 and 3 show the Template Block 1 blocks for the Yosemite National Park quilt (C/B and D/C) and the New River Gorge National Park wall hanging (A/B, B/A, C/A, and D/C). Note which fabric name is in the Template A position (for both half- and quarter-curve blocks) prior to piecing.

Figure 2   *Figure 3*

For the New River Gorge National Park wall hanging, instructions are to piece together: A/B + B/A + A4. Refer to Figure 4 for an example of how this is shown in a diagram.

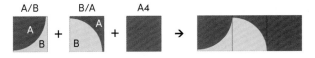

Figure 4

Piecing with HSTs and HRTs

HSTs and HRTs are frequently rotated in each pattern and are listed in the correct direction for piecing. Piecing instructions for HSTs are referred to by orientation, A/D or D/A, with the first letter being the fabric on the left when sewn. For the Joshua Tree National Park quilt, instructions are to piece together: D/A + HST 2 + A/D. Refer to Figure 5 for an example of how this is shown in a diagram.

Figure 5

HRTs are referred to similarly as HSTs, but also include the R/L orientation designation. For example, Figure 6 shows a portion of Row 6 for the Rocky Mountain National Park quilt with instructions to piece together: C/A (right) + A/C (left) + C14 + C/A + A/C (left). Note the first letter is the fabric on the left when sewn.

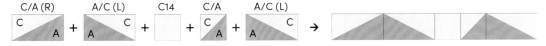

Figure 6

Abbreviations Used in Piecing Instructions

- (R): Right Orientation - For HRTs and Yosemite National Park Template Block 2
- (L): Left Orientation - For HRTs and Yosemite National Park Template Block 2

Some projects have multiple HRTs and Template Blocks and are referred to as:

- (1R): HRT 1 - Right Orientation
- (1L): HRT 1 - Left Orientation
- (1): HST 1 or Template Block 1

- (2R): HRT 2 - Right Orientation
- (2L): HRT 2 - Left Orientation
- (2): HST 2 or Template Block 2

MATCHING SEAMS

Matching seams can be a frustrating process, even for seasoned quilters. There are two methods for matching seams: nesting and using a stay stitch.

Nesting

Nesting seams simply means to press the seam allowance to one side for one unit, then in the opposite direction for the second unit, so the fabrics interlock when sewing the two units together. This helps reduce bulk where several seams meet and helps with seam alignment, allowing the seams to fit together like a puzzle, as shown in Figure 1.

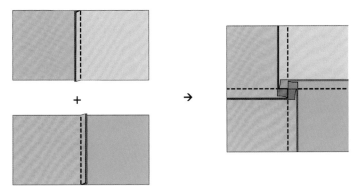

Figure 1

Stay Stitch

Using a stay stitch involves sewing a short stitch over the matching seams prior to sewing two entire rows together. Figure 2 shows two partial rows of the Glacier Bay National Park quilt. To match the seams of Row 3A + 4A, place the two rows right sides together and pin where the seams match, then stitch a short .25 in. (.6 cm) seam allowance over the seams. Open the rows to check for alignment as shown in Figure 3. If the seams aren't matched, use a seam ripper to remove the stay stitches, realign, pin, and stitch together again. Once the seam alignment is correct, sew a .25 in. (.6 cm) seam allowance across the entire row, slowly stitching over the previous stitches.

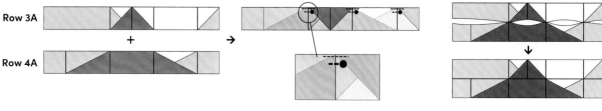

Figure 2   Figure 3

Pressing Seams

After piecing each block, always press your seams. Pressing to one side is believed to help reinforce the seams and strengthen the quilt, while pressing open creates flatter seams and reduces bulk when several seams come together in one spot. Regardless of which you choose, make sure to use an up-and-down motion while pressing rather than the back-and-forth motion of ironing to avoid stretching the fabric. I pressed my seams open for the projects in this book, but if you plan on nesting your seams, press to one side.

ASSEMBLING YOUR QUILT

PREPARING THE BACKING

All backing yardage in this book allows for 4 in. (10.2 cm) overage on all sides and assumes fabric is nondirectional. For throws and smaller, backing yardage is cut in half lengthwise. For bed quilts, backing yardage is cut into thirds lengthwise. Piece backing cuts together using a .5 in. (1.3 cm) seam allowance and ensure that it is 4 in. (10.2 cm) larger than your quilt top on all sides. Press your backing prior to making your quilt sandwich.

BUILDING A QUILT SANDWICH

If you're sending your quilt to a longarmer (a person who finishes your quilt using a special sewing machine called a longarm), you do not need to make a quilt sandwich. To finish your quilt at home:

1 Make sure you press all quilt top seams and trim long threads.

2 Lay your backing on a large surface, right side down. Use pins to secure your backing to the carpet or use painter's tape to secure it to a smooth surface. Make sure your backing is taut and there are no wrinkles.

3 Place the batting on top of the backing and use your hands to smooth out any creases so it lies flat. As with your quilt backing, the batting should also be 4 in. (10.2 cm) larger than your quilt top on all sides.

To make a quilt sandwich using pins:

4 Place your freshly pressed quilt top right side up on top of your batting, ensuring you have 4 in. (10.2 cm) overage of batting on each side of the top. Smooth out any creases from the top.

5 If you have a specific quilting design planned, mark your quilt top with either a water-soluble marker or a hera marker. (I like to mark my tops prior to pinning so that I can place my pins away from any marked quilting lines.)

6 Grab your curved quilting safety pins and, starting at the center of the quilt, baste the pieces together by placing the pins approximately 4 in. (10.2 cm) from each other. To reduce time and prevent sore fingers, store your pins open when you remove them.

To make a quilt sandwich using spray baste:

4 Roll up your batting from either the top or the bottom width and set aside.

5 Place your freshly pressed quilt top on the floor, right side up, and roll it up as well and set it aside.

6 In a well-ventilated space, spray the backing all over, holding the adhesive 12 in. (30.5 cm) away from the backing. Roll the batting back on top of the backing, using your hands to smooth it out.

7 Spray the adhesive all over the batting. Unroll your quilt top on top of the sprayed batting, ensuring there is 4 in. (10.2 cm) backing/batting overage on each side of the quilt top. Smooth out any wrinkles with your hands.

8 If you have a specific quilting design planned, mark your quilt top with either a water-soluble marker or a hera marker.

QUILTING

Quilting is the patterned stitching that secures all of your pieces (quilt top, batting, and backing) together. Quilting can be done on a domestic sewing machine, by hand, or by a longarm quilter. Depending on the machine, longarm quilters can sew custom designs or use a pantograph to quilt a preexisting design. Longarm quilting can be a time-saver and a great way to incorporate a unique and complicated design on your quilt top.

Whether you choose to send your piece out to a longarm quilter or quilt at home, there are many quilting designs available to add a decorative stitch and secure all your quilt layers. Longarm quilters will have pantographs for you to choose from or suggest designer sites that have additional options. For quilting at home, I recommend checking out Jacquie Gering's book, *Walk: Master Machine Quilting with Your Walking Foot*. This book has incredible design suggestions, from simple to complicated, and will teach you how to mark your quilts to create each design. If you're using your machine to quilt, make sure you switch to your walking foot.

TRIMMING AND SQUARING

After your quilt has been quilted, use your ruler, rotary cutter, and cutting mat to square up your quilt corners to each have 90-degree angles. Trim the excess batting and backing around your quilt top.

BINDING

Binding is the border or "frame" of your quilt. Binding can be done with any fabric you choose—it can be a contrasting fabric or one of the colors you've used in the pattern. It all depends on your taste. Making and attaching binding is one of those steps in the quilting process that takes time to learn and a lot of practice, but once it clicks, you'll be a pro. That being said, I learned how to make and attach binding by watching videos, so if these instructions don't quite make sense, I highly recommend looking online for video tutorials.

1 To make your binding, first trim any selvage edges from your strips. Next, place a strip right side down and fold back the top right corner 45 degrees and mark a crease, as shown in Figure 1.

2 Place the creased strip perpendicular to another strip, right sides together. Sew directly on the creased line, then trim a .25 in. (.6 cm) seam allowance, as shown in Figure 2.

3 Press the seams open. Continue piecing strips together until you have one long strip. Fold the strip in half lengthwise, wrong sides together, and press to create your binding, as shown in Figure 3.

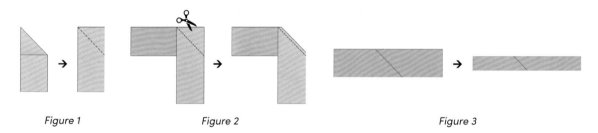

Figure 1   Figure 2   Figure 3

4 Lay your binding on top of your quilt, with the edges of your quilt lined up with the raw edges of your binding. To make binding Tail 1, leave at least 8 in. (20.3 cm) of binding from your sewing starting point. Find the halfway point between the corners of your quilt and sew on your binding using a .25 in. (.6 cm) seam allowance. When you are .25 in. (.6 cm) away from the corner, lift your sewing machine foot, turn, and sew a 45-degree angle to the corner, as shown in Figure 4.

5 Turn up your binding, making a 45-degree angle, as shown in Figure 5.

6 Fold down your binding, keeping the folded 45-degree binding triangle underneath, as shown in Figure 6. Align the raw edges of your binding with the raw edges of your quilt.

7 Starting at the top corner, continue sewing your binding to your quilt, as shown in Figure 7.

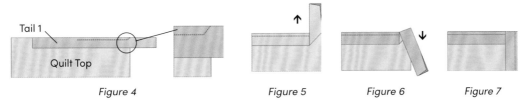

Figure 4   Figure 5   Figure 6   Figure 7

8 Stop stitching when you are at least 12 in. (30.5 cm) away from where you started, as shown in Figure 8. Leave at least 8 in. (20.3 cm) of extra binding for Tail 2, and trim off any excess binding length.

9 Align your binding tails on top of each other, overlapping Tail 1 and Tail 2. Open your excess binding piece or grab a fabric scrap and cut it to 2.5 in. (6.3 cm), and center it on the overlapped tails, as shown in Figure 9. This excess binding piece will be the width of your binding, which is 2.5 in. (6.3 cm).

10 Trim each tail so that they overlap by 2.5 in. (6.3 cm), as shown in Figure 10.

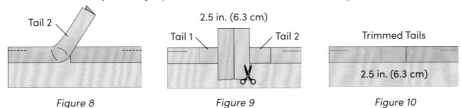

Figure 8   Figure 9   Figure 10

11 Open Tail 2 and place it right side up on a flat surface. Open Tail 1 and place it right side down, as shown in Figure 11.

12 Place your binding tails together perpendicularly, right sides together, pin, and sew a diagonal line from corner to corner, as shown in Figure 12. Trim a .25 in. (.6 cm) seam allowance and press the seams open.

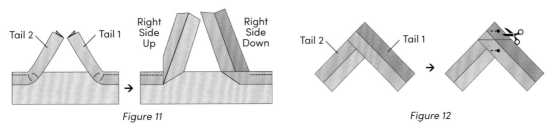

Figure 11   Figure 12

13 Straighten and refold your pieced binding and finish stitching it to the front of your quilt, as shown in Figure 13.

14 Flip over your quilt so that the backing is face up, and fold your binding over and press to create a creased line. Fold each corner to 45 degrees, as shown in Figure 14. To finish your quilt, hand stitch or machine sew your binding to the back.

Figure 13   Figure 14

* Washing Your Quilt Use cold water on a delicate cycle with a gentle detergent. Tumble dry on low heat or hang to dry.

FINISHING A PILLOW COVER

For the back of the pillow, you can use one of the fabrics from the front of the pillow or choose something completely different—it's up to you (if you use one of the fabrics from the front, be sure to get the extra yardage listed under Pillow Cover). Cut two equally sized fabric pieces according to the cutting instructions of the project. You will have a left piece and a right piece. Place the left piece wrong side up and fold the right edge over .25 in. (.6 cm) and press, then fold it over .25 in. (.6 cm) again and press to create a finished edge. Stitch along the edge, as shown in Figure 1. Repeat with the right piece, folding and stitching on the left edge.

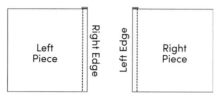

Figure 1

BINDING

To add binding to your pillow, place your quilted pillow top face down, then place the left and right pieces on top, right sides up (wrong sides together). Align the left piece with the left edge, and the right piece with the right edge, leaving an overlap of several inches in the middle, as shown in Figure 2. Stitch .25 in. (.6 cm) around the edges of the quilt, then trim the excess corner fabric to reduce bulk, as shown in Figure 3. Bind as desired.

If you prefer not to use binding, place your quilted pillow top face up, then place the left and right pieces on top, wrong sides up (right sides together). Align the left piece with the left edge, right piece with the right edge, leaving an overlap of several inches in the middle, as shown in Figure 2. Stitch .25 in. (.6 cm) around the edges of the quilt, then trim excess corner fabric to reduce bulk, as shown in Figure 3. Turn your pillow top right side out and use a point turner to sharpen your corners.

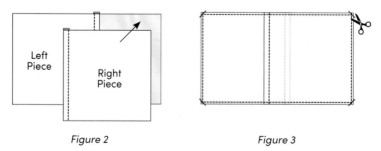

Figure 2   Figure 3

Your finished pillow will look best with an insert 1–2 in. (2.5–5 cm) larger all around, rather than the exact size of your pillow cover.

FINISHING A WALL HANGING

Wall hangings need support on the corners to lie flat. Before you attach your binding to the finished piece, cut two 5 in. (12.7 cm) squares, then fold each in half diagonally, wrong sides together, as shown in Figure 1. Place the triangles on the back in the top corners of your binding and stitch around the sides and top, as shown in Figure 2. Attach the binding as usual. Use a dowel to hang.

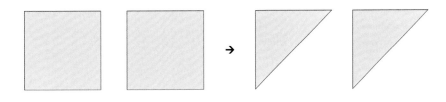

Figure 1

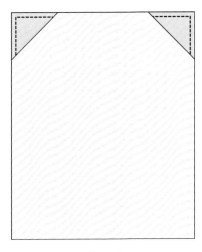

Figure 2

Decor

White Sands

NEW MEXICO

Covering more than 145,000 acres of wavelike dunes, this park in New Mexico is the world's largest gypsum dune field. Formed after the evaporation of an ancient sea, the "sand" at White Sands National Park is not like typical beach sand; instead, it dissolves in water and doesn't absorb heat from the sun, making it cool to walk on. Rain in the mountains causes the gypsum to dissolve and run down into the fully enclosed Tularosa Basin, keeping the sand within the park. Gypsum is a naturally clear substance, but scratches on the crystals reflect sunlight and make them appear white. With moonlit hikes and designated sledding dunes, this is truly a unique park to visit. This pillow features a simple dune design using half-rectangle triangles and half-square triangles in five soft colors to capture the light and shadows of the shifting dunes.

Finished Measurements | Height: 20 in. (50.8 cm) Width: 20 in. (50.8 cm)

FABRIC: Art Gallery Fabrics *Pure Solids*, 100% cotton
(width: 44 in. [111.75 cm], weight per yard: 4.7 oz)

A (Morning Frost) – .33 yard

B (Honeydew) – .25 yard

C (White Linen) – .25 yard

D (Northern Waters) – .125 yard

E (Blushing) – .125 yard

BACKING: Scrap fabric or muslin – .875 yard

PILLOW COVER (BACK): Any desired fabric – .5 yard

BINDING: Any desired fabric – .25 yard

NOTIONS: Batting – 28 in. x 28 in. (71.1 cm x 71.1 cm)

22 in. (55.9 cm) square pillow form

Cutting Instructions | PILLOW

Note: For more information on cutting and assembling blocks, see p. 14.

A (Morning Frost)

Cut one 10 in. (25.4 cm) x WOF strip. Subcut:

2 - 8.5 in. x 12.5 in. (21.6 cm x 31.75 cm) [A3]

2 - 5 in. x 10 in. (12.7 cm x 25.4 cm) [A1]

1 - 5 in. x 5 in. (12.7 cm x 12.7 cm) [A2]

B (Honeydew)

Cut one 5 in. (12.7 cm) x WOF strip. Subcut:

1 - 5 in. x 10 in. (12.7 cm x 25.4 cm) [B1]

2 - 5 in. x 5 in. (12.7 cm x 12.7 cm) [B2]

1 - 4.5 in. x 4.5 in. (11.4 cm x 11.4 cm) [B5]

1 - 3 in. x 3 in. (7.6 cm x 7.6 cm) [B3]

1 - 2.5 in. x 2.5 in. (6.3 cm x 6.3 cm) [B4]

C (White Linen)

Cut one 6 in. (15.2 cm) x WOF strip. Subcut:

2 - 3 in. x 6 in. (7.6 cm x 15.2 cm) [C2]

1 - 5 in. x 10 in. (12.7 cm x 25.4 cm) [C1]

1 - 5 in. x 5 in. (12.7 cm x 12.7 cm) [C3]

1 - 4.5 in. x 8.5 in. (11.4 cm x 21.6 cm) [C5]

2 - 3 in. x 3 in. (7.6 cm x 7.6 cm) [C4]

2 - 2.5 in. x 2.5 in. (6.3 cm x 6.3 cm) [C6]

D (Nothern Waters)

Cut one 3 in. (7.6 cm) x WOF strip. Subcut:

1 - 3 in. x 6 in. (7.6 cm x 15.2 cm) [D1]

1 - 3 in. x 3 in. (7.6 cm x 7.6 cm) [D2]

1 - 2.5 in. x 2.5 in. (6.3 cm x 6.3 cm) [D3]

E (Blushing)

Cut one 3 in. (7.6 cm) x WOF strip. Subcut:

1 - 3 in. x 6 in. (7.6 cm x 15.2 cm) [E1]

2 - 3 in. x 3 in. (7.6 cm x 7.6 cm) [E2]

1 - 2.5 in. x 4.5 in. (6.3 cm x 11.4 cm) [E3]

BINDING *Cut three 2.5 in. (6.3 cm) x WOF strips of the binding fabric.*

PILLOW COVER *Cut two 15 in. x 20 in. (38 cm x 50.8 cm) pieces of the pillow cover fabric.*

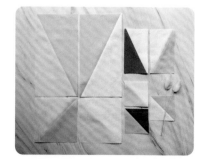

Block Assembly

1) To make the HSTs, pair each A2, B2, C3, B3, C4, D2, and E2 square with its corresponding square, as shown in Figure 1. Refer to Figure 1 to determine the required amount and fabric combinations of HSTs. *See Half-Square Triangles (p. 19) for two-at-a-time HST piecing and trimming instructions.* Trim HST 1 to 4.5 in. x 4.5 in. (11.4 cm x 11.4 cm) and HST 2 to 2.5 in. x 2.5 in. (6.3 cm x 6.3 cm).

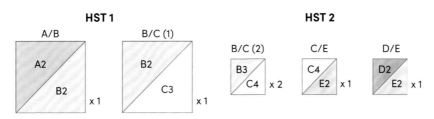

Figure 1

2) HRTs are sewn in two different orientations (right and left). Organize each A1, B1, C1, C2, D1, and E1 rectangle into piles, referring to Figure 2 to determine the required amount for each right/left orientation. Cut each rectangle in half diagonally, paying close attention to the direction each is cut. Keep each HRT in its right/left orientation stack.

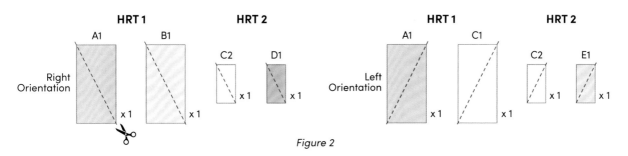

Figure 2

3) Pair each cut triangle with its corresponding cut triangle, as shown in Figure 3. Refer to Figure 3 to determine the required amount and fabric combinations of the HRTs. *See Half-Rectangle Triangles (p. 16) for HRT piecing and trimming instructions.* Trim HRT 1 to 4.5 in. x 8.5 in. (11.4 cm x 21.6 cm) and HRT 2 to 2.5 in. x 4.5 in. (6.3 cm x 11.4 cm).

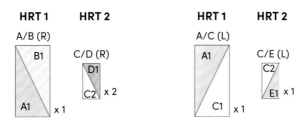

Figure 3

Quilt Assembly

1) To make Block 1, first piece together A/B + C/A (left), then piece A3 on top, as shown in Figure 4.

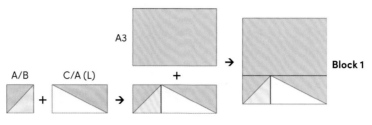

Figure 4

2) To make Block 2, piece together A3 + Block 1, as shown in Figure 5.

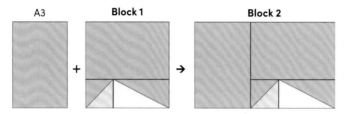

Figure 5

3) To make Block 3, piece together A/B (right) + B/C (HST 1) + C5, as shown in Figure 6.

Figure 6

4) To make Block 4, first piece together B4 + B/C (HST 2) + C6 + C/D (right) + E/C (left) + C6, and B/C (HST 2) + C/D (right) + D3 + D/E + E3 + E/C into rows. Next, piece these rows together, as shown in Figure 7.

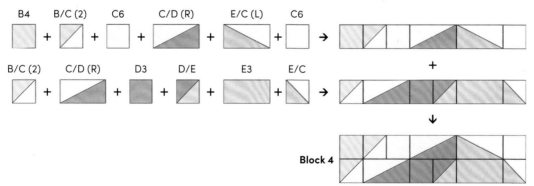

Figure 7

5) To make Block 5, piece together B5 + Block 4, as shown in Figure 8.

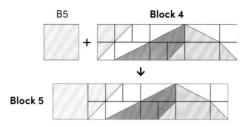

Figure 8

6) Piece together Block 2 + Block 3 + Block 5, as shown in Figure 9.

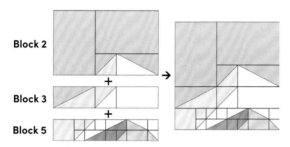

Figure 9

To finish your White Sands pillow, see Assembling Your Quilt (p. 23) and Finishing a Pillow (p. 26) or turn this project into a wall hanging (p. 27).

White Sands Quilt Pattern

Redwood

CALIFORNIA

Redwood National Park, in Northern California, is home to the world's tallest trees, some nearly 380 feet tall. While the average life span of a redwood is 500 to 700 years, some are more than 2,000 years old. During the dry season, redwoods create their own moisture by trapping fog on their uppermost needles. These water droplets are then absorbed by the tree, and any leftover moisture will fall to the forest floor, with a large redwood tree holding about 34,000 pounds of water. Because Redwood National Park is located in a temperate rainforest, visitors can enjoy hiking, biking, fishing, wildlife sightings, and 40 miles of coastline throughout the year. This pillow features the rugged texture and rich colors of the bark found on these ancient trees, which can be up to 12 inches thick.

Finished Measurements | Height: 16 in. (40.6 cm) Width: 24 in. (61 cm)

FABRIC: Art Gallery Fabrics *Pure Solids*, 100% cotton
(width: 44 in. [111.75 cm], weight per yard: 4.7 oz)

■ **A** (Coffee Bean) – .33 yard

■ **B** (Chocolate) – .25 yard

■ **C** (Toasty Walnut) – .25 yard

■ **D** (Apple Cider) – .125 yard

BACKING: Scrap fabric or muslin – .67 yard

PILLOW COVER (BACK): Any desired fabric – .5 yard

BINDING: Any desired fabric – .25 yard

NOTIONS: Batting – 32 in. x 24 in. (81.3 cm x 61 cm)

26 in. x 18 in. (66 cm x 45.7 cm) pillow form

Cutting Instructions | PILLOW

Note: For more information on cutting and assembling blocks, see p. 14.

■ A (Coffee Bean)

Cut one 3.25 in. (8.2 cm) x WOF strip. Subcut:

1 - 3.25 in. x 8 in.
(8.2 cm x 20.3 cm) [A17]

1 - 2 in. x 3.25 in.
(5.1 cm x 8.2 cm) [A16]

1 - 1.75 in. x 3.25 in.
(4.4 cm x 8.2 cm) [A20]

1 - 2.75 in. x 6.25 in.
(7 cm x 15.9 cm) [A8]

1 - 2 in. x 2.75 in.
(5.1 cm x 7 cm) [A14]

1 - 2.25 in. x 7.5 in.
(5.7 cm x 19 cm) [A5]

1 - 2.25 in. x 7.25 in.
(5.7 cm x 18.4 cm) [A18]

1 - 2 in. x 2.25 in.
(5.1 cm x 5.7 cm) [A19]

Cut one 1.75 in. (4.4 cm) x WOF strip. Subcut:

1 - 1.75 in. x 9.5 in.
(4.4 cm x 24 cm) [A10]

1 - 1.75 in. x 5.5 in.
(4.4 cm x 14 cm) [A11]

1 - 1.75 in. x 5 in.
(4.4 cm x 12.7 cm) [A12]

1 - 1.75 in. x 16.5 in.
(4.4 cm x 42 cm) [A21]

Cut one 1.5 in. (3.8 cm) x WOF strip. Subcut:

2 - 1.5 in. x 6.5 in.
(3.8 cm x 16.5 cm) [A3]

1 - 1.5 in. x 12.75 in.
(3.8 cm x 32.4 cm) [A7]

1 - 2 in. x 1.5 in.
(5.1 cm x 3.8 cm) [A13]

Cut one 1.25 in. (3.2 cm) x WOF strip. Subcut:

1 - 1.25 in. x 7 in.
(3.2 cm x 17.8 cm) [A1]

1 - 1.25 in. x 6.5 in.
(3.2 cm x 16.5 cm) [A2]

1 - 1.25 in. x 8.25 in.
(3.2 cm x 21 cm) [A6]

1 - 1.25 in. x 9.5 in.
(3.2 cm x 24 cm) [A9]

1 - 2 in. x 1.25 in.
(5.1 cm x 3.2 cm) [A15]

1 - 1 in. x 6.25 in.
(2.5 cm x 15.9 cm) [A4]

■ B (Chocolate)

Cut one 2.25 in. (5.7 cm) x WOF strip. Subcut:

1 - 2.25 in. x 4.25 in.
(5.7 cm x 10.8 cm) [B11]

1 - 2 in. x 10.5 in.
(5.1 cm x 26.7 cm) [B10]

1 - 2 in. x 9.5 in.
(5.1 cm x 24 cm) [B13]

1 - 2 in. x 16.5 in.
(5.1 cm x 42 cm) [B14]

Cut one 2 in. (5.1 cm) x WOF strip. Subcut:

1 - 2 in. x 5 in.
(5.1 cm x 12.7 cm) [B8]

1 - 2 in. x 6.25 in.
(5.1 cm x 15.9 cm) [B9]

1 - 1.75 in. x 2 in.
(4.4 cm x 5.1 cm) [B12]

1 - 1.5 in. x 6.25 in.
(3.8 cm x 15.9 cm) [B6]

1 - 1.25 in. x 6.5 in.
(3.2 cm x 16.5 cm) [B3]

1 - 1.25 in. x 12.75 in.
(3.2 cm x 32.4 cm) [B5]

Cut two 1 in. (2.5 cm)
x WOF strips. Subcut:

1 - 1 in. x 7 in.
(2.5 cm x 17.8 cm) [B1]

3 - 1 in. x 6.5 in.
(2.5 cm x 16.5 cm) [B2]

2 - 1 in. x 6.25 in.
(2.5 cm x 15.9 cm) [B4]

2 - 1 in. x 6 in.
(2.5 cm x 15.2 cm) [B7]

 **C** (Toasty Walnut)

Cut one 1.5 in. (3.8 cm)
x WOF strip. Subcut:

1 - 1.5 in. x 6.5 in.
(3.8 cm x 16.5 cm) [C1]

1 - 1.5 in. x 7.5 in.
(3.8 cm x 19 cm) [C2]

1 - 1.5 in. x 9.25 in.
(3.8 cm x 23.5 cm) [C7]

1 - 1.5 in. x 2.25 in.
(3.8 cm x 5.7 cm) [C8]

1 - 1.25 in. x 9.5 in.
(3.2 cm x 24 cm) [C3]

1 - 1 in. x 6 in.
(2.5 cm x 15.2 cm) [C4]

Cut one 2 in. (5.1 cm)
x WOF strip. Subcut:

1 - 2 in. x 9.75 in.
(5.1 cm x 24.7 cm) [C5]

1 - 1.25 in. x 2 in.
(3.2 cm x 2.5 cm) [C6]

D (Apple Cider)

Cut one 1.75 in. (4.4 cm)
x WOF strip. Subcut:

1 - 1.75 in. x 9.25 in.
(4.4 cm x 23.5 cm) [D4]

1 - 1.75 in. x 2.25 in.
(4.4 cm x 5.7 cm) [D5]

1 - 1.75 in. x 16.5 in.
(4.4 cm x 42 cm) [D6]

1 - 1.5 in. x 8.25 in.
(3.8 cm x 21 cm) [D1]

Cut one 1.25 in. (3.2 cm)
x WOF strip. Subcut:

1 - 1.25 in. x 6 in.
(3.2 cm x 15.2 cm) [D3]

2 - 1 in. x 6.25 in.
(2.5 cm x 15.9 cm) [D2]

BINDING Cut three 2.5 in.
(6.3 cm) x WOF strips of the
binding fabric.

PILLOW COVER Cut two
16 in. x 17 in. (40.6 cm
x 43.2 cm) pieces of the
pillow cover fabric.

Quilt Assembly

1) **To make Block 1,** piece together A1 + B1, as shown in Figure 1. To make Block 2, piece together C1 + B2, as shown in Figure 2. To make Block 3A, piece together A2 + B3, as shown in Figure 3. To make Block 3B, piece together B2 + A3, as shown in Figure 4.

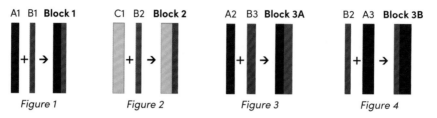

Figure 1   Figure 2   Figure 3   Figure 4

2) **To make Block 4,** piece together B4 + A4 + B4, as shown in Figure 5. To make Block 5, piece together A5 + C2, as shown in Figure 6. To make Block 6, piece together D1 + A6, as shown in Figure 7. To make Block 7, piece together B2 + A3, as shown in Figure 8.

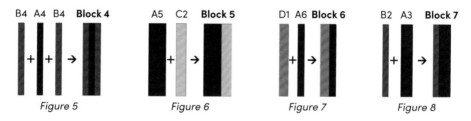

Figure 5   Figure 6   Figure 7   Figure 8

3) **To make Block 8,** piece together A7 + B5, as shown in Figure 9. To make Block 9A, piece together A8 + D2, as shown in Figure 10. To make Block 9B, piece together A9 + C3 + A10, as shown in Figure 11.

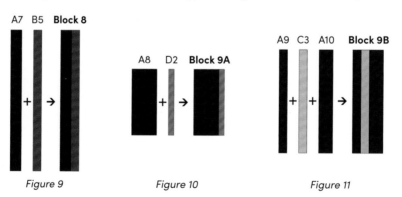

Figure 9   Figure 10   Figure 11

4) **To make Block 10,** piece together D2 + B6, as shown in Figure 12. To make Block 11, piece together D3 + B7, as shown in Figure 13. To make Block 12, piece together B7 + C4, as shown in Figure 14.

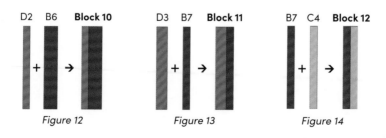

Figure 12   Figure 13   Figure 14

5) To make Row 1, piece together A11 + Block 1 + A12, as shown in Figure 15.
To make Row 2, piece together C5 + Block 2 + C6, as shown in Figure 16.
To make Row 3, piece together A13 + Block 3A + A14 + Block 3B + A15, as shown in Figure 17.
To make Row 4, piece together B8 + Block 4 + B9, as shown in Figure 18.

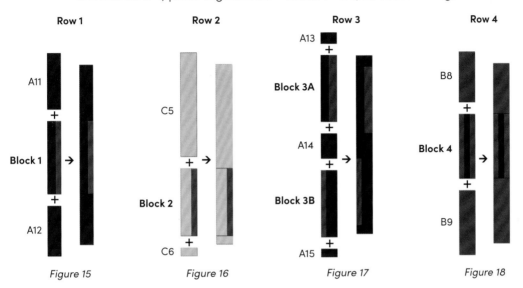

Figure 15   Figure 16   Figure 17   Figure 18

6) To make Row 5, piece together A16 + Block 5 + A17, as shown in Figure 19. To make Row 6, piece together A18 + Block 6 + A19, as shown in Figure 20. To make Row 7, piece together B10 + Block 7, as shown in Figure 21. To make Row 8, piece together Block 8 + B11, as shown in Figure 22.

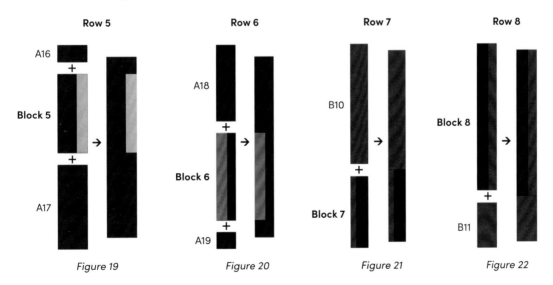

Figure 19   Figure 20   Figure 21   Figure 22

7) To make Row 9, piece together A20 + Block 9A + Block 9B, as shown in Figure 23. To make Row 10, piece together B12 + Block 10 + B13, as shown in Figure 24. To make Row 11, piece together D4 + Block 11 + D5, as shown in Figure 25. To make Row 12, piece together C7 + Block 12 + C8, as shown in Figure 26.

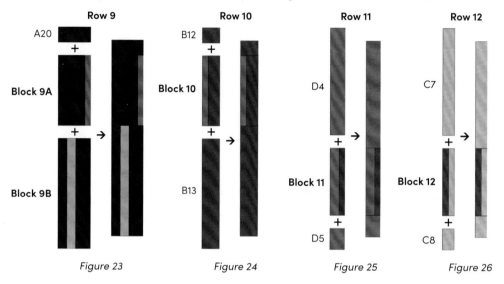

Figure 23   Figure 24   Figure 25   Figure 26

8) Piece the rows and remaining pieces together in the order shown in Figure 27.

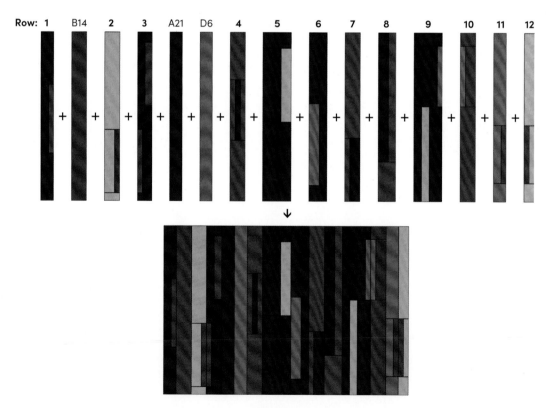

Figure 27

To finish your Redwood pillow, see Assembling Your Quilt (p. 23) and Finishing a Pillow Cover (p. 26) or turn this project into a wall hanging (see p. 27).

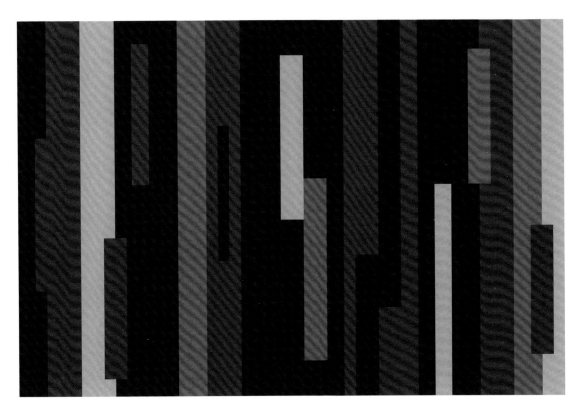

Redwood Quilt Pattern

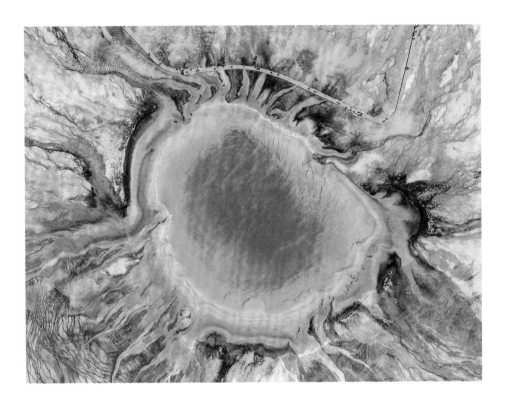

Yellowstone

WYOMING

The first National Park in the United States, Yellowstone is located on 2.2 million acres in Wyoming, Montana, and Idaho. This park has dramatic canyons, lush forests, and nearly 1,000 miles of hiking trails, 290 waterfalls, and the famous geyser, Old Faithful, that erupts approximately seventeen times per day and whose plume can reach heights of 184 feet. Yellowstone is also known for its more than 10,000 geothermal features, including the Grand Prismatic Spring. Named after its striking colors, it is the largest hot spring in the United States. Because it sits on the active Yellowstone Volcano, visitors are advised to stay on designated trails and boardwalks as thin surface crust can quickly give way to acidic groundwater that can reach 250°F. This pillow features vibrant fabrics in reds, oranges, yellows, greens, and blues to capture the vivid colors of the Grand Prismatic Spring and is a great starter project if you are new to quilting.

Finished Measurements | Height: 12 in. (30.5 cm) Width: 22 in. (55.9 cm)

FABRIC: Art Gallery Fabrics *Pure Solids*, 100% cotton
(width: 44 in. [111.75 cm], weight per yard: 4.7 oz)

A (Dark Citron) – .125 yard

B (Turmeric) – .125 yard

C (Autumnal) – .125 yard

D (Desert Dunes) – .125 yard

E (Eucalyptus) – .125 yard

F (Periwinkle) – .125 yard

G (Tranquil Waters) – .125 yard

H (Aero Blue) – .125 yard

I (Denim Blue) – .125 yard

J (Night Sea) – .125 yard

K (Nocturnal) – .125 yard

BACKING: Scrap fabric or muslin – .5 yard

PILLOW COVER (BACK): Any desired fabric – .375 yard

BINDING: Any desired fabric – .25 yard

NOTIONS: Batting – 30 in. x 20 in. (76.2 cm x 50.8 cm)

24 in. x 14 in. (61 cm x 35.5 cm) pillow form

Cutting Instructions | PILLOW

Note: For more information on cutting and assembling blocks, see p. 14.

A (Dark Citron)

Cut one 2 in. (5.1 cm) x WOF strip. Subcut:

10 – 2 in. x 3.5 in. (5.1 cm x 8.9 cm) [A1]

2 – 2 in. x 2.5 in. (5.1 cm x 6.3 cm) [A2]

B (Turmeric)

Cut one 2 in. (5.1 cm) x WOF strip. Subcut:

8 – 2 in. x 3.5 in. (5.1 cm x 8.9 cm) [B1]

2 – 1.5 in. x 2 in. (3.8 cm x 2.5 cm) [B2]

C (Autumnal)

Cut one 2 in. (5.1 cm) x WOF strip. Subcut:

4 – 2 in. x 3.5 in. (5.1 cm x 8.9 cm) [C1]

2 – 2 in. x 2.5 in. (5.1 cm x 6.3 cm) [C2]

D (Desert Dunes)

Cut one 2 in. (5.1 cm) x WOF strip. Subcut:

2 – 2 in. x 3.5 in. (5.1 cm x 8.9 cm) [D1]

2 – 1.5 in. x 2 in. (3.8 cm x 2.5 cm) [D2]

E (Eucalyptus)

Cut one 2.5 in. (6.3 cm) x WOF strip. Subcut:

1 – 1.5 in. x 2.5 in. (3.8 cm 6.3 cm) [E3]

10 – 2 in. x 3.5 in. (5.1 cm x 8.9 cm) [E2]

2 – 2 in. x 2.5 in. (5.1 cm x 6.3 cm) [E1]

F (Periwinkle)

Cut one 1.5 in. (3.8 cm) x WOF strip. Subcut:

2 – 1.5 in. x 2 in. (3.8 cm x 5.1 cm) [F1]

G (Tranquil Waters)

Cut one 2 in. (5.1 cm) x WOF strip. Subcut:

2 – 2 in. x 3.5 in. (5.1 cm x 8.9 cm) [G1]

H (Aero Blue)

Cut one 2 in. (5.1 cm) x WOF strip. Subcut:

2 – 2 in. x 5.5 in. (5.1 cm x 14 cm) [H1]

I (Denim Blue)

Cut one 2 in. (5.1 cm) x WOF strip. Subcut:

2 – 2 in. x 7.5 in. (5.1 cm x 19 cm) [I1]

J (Night Sea)

Cut one 2 in. (5.1 cm) x WOF strip. Subcut:

2 – 2 in. x 9.5 in. (5.1 cm x 24 cm) [J1]

K (Nocturnal)

Cut one 1.5 in. (3.8 cm) x WOF strip. Subcut:

1 – 1.5 in. x 10.5 in. (3.8 cm x 26.7 cm) [K1]

BINDING *Cut two 2.5 in. (6.3 cm) x WOF strips of the binding fabric.*

PILLOW COVER *Cut two 12 in. x 15 in. (30.5 cm x 38 cm) pieces of the pillow cover fabric.*

Quilt Assembly

1) To make Rows 1–8, piece blocks together in the order shown in Figure 1. Make two of each of Rows 1–7, and one Row 8.

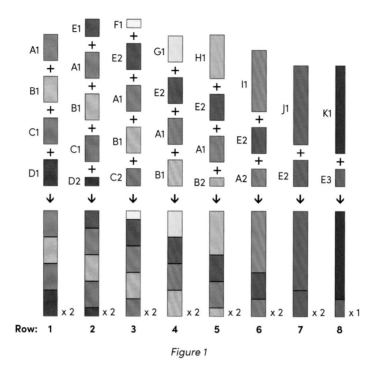

Figure 1

2) Piece together Rows 1–8 + Rows 7–1, as shown in Figure 2.

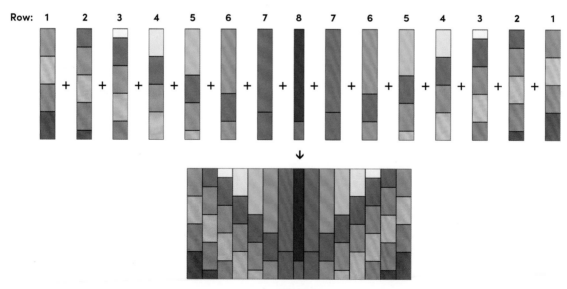

Figure 2

To finish your Yellowstone pillow, see Assembling Your Quilt (p. 23) and Finishing a Pillow Cover (p. 26) or turn this project into a wall hanging (see p. 27).

Yellowstone Quilt Pattern

Congaree

SOUTH CAROLINA

Located on 26,000 acres inside the Congaree River floodplain in South Carolina, Congaree National Park is home to some of the tallest trees in Eastern North America, with an average height of about 100 feet. Visitors can take a walk along the 2.4-mile Boardwalk Trail, enjoy a nighttime hike known as the "owl prowl" to hear barred owls and see a glow-in-the-dark fungus that grows on trees, or between mid-May and mid-June, observe millions of fireflies synchronize and flash together as they search for a mate. This pillow recreates the 500-year-old bald cypress trees and their reflection in this bottomland forest using half-rectangle triangles in rich forest colors.

Finished Measurements | Height: 20 in. (50.8 cm) Width: 20 in. (50.8 cm)

FABRIC: Art Gallery Fabrics *Pure Solids*, 100% cotton
(width: 44 in. [111.75 cm], weight per yard: 4.7 oz)

A (Golden Bronze) – .33 yard

B (Forest Night) – .33 yard

C (Pacific) – .125 yard

BACKING: Scrap fabric or muslin – .875 yard

PILLOW COVER (BACK):
Any desired fabric – .5 yard

BINDING: Any desired fabric – .25 yard

NOTIONS: Batting – 28 in. x 28 in. (71.1 cm x 71.1 cm)

22 in. (55.9 cm) square pillow form

Cutting Instructions | PILLOW

Note: For more information on cutting and assembling blocks, see p. 14.

A (Golden Bronze)

Cut two 3.5 in. (8.9 cm) x WOF strips. Subcut:

6 - 3.5 in. x 8 in. (8.9 cm x 20.3 cm) [A1]

3 - 3 in. x 6.5 in. (7.6 cm x 16.5 cm) [A3]

Cut one 3 in. (7.6 cm) x WOF strip. Subcut:

3 - 3 in. x 13.75 in. (7.6 cm x 35 cm) [A2]

B (Forest Night)

Cut one 3.5 in. (8.9 cm) x WOF strip. Subcut:

5 - 3.5 in. x 8 in. (8.9 cm x 20.3 cm) [B1]

Cut one 4.75 in. (12 cm) x WOF strip. Subcut:

2 - 4.75 in. x 7.75 in. (12 cm x 19.7 cm) [B4]

1 - 3.5 in. x 8 in. (8.9 cm x 20.3 cm) [B1 – 6 total]

2 - 2.5 in. x 7.75 in. (6.3 cm x 19.7 cm) [B3]

2 - .75 in. x 6.5 in. (1.9 cm x 16.5 cm) [B2]

6 - .75 in. x 2 in. (1.9 cm x 5.1 cm) [B5]

C (Pacific)

Cut two 1.25 in. (3.2 cm) x WOF strips. Subcut:

3 - 1.25 in. x 20.5 in. (3.2 cm x 52 cm) [C1]

BINDING *Cut three 2.5 in. (6.3 cm) x WOF strips of the binding fabric.*

PILLOW COVER *Cut two 15 in. x 20 in. (38 cm x 50.8 cm) pieces of the pillow cover fabric.*

Block Assembly

1) HRTs are sewn in two different orientations (right and left).
Organize each A1 and B1 rectangle into piles, referring to Figure 1 to determine the required amount for each right/left orientation. Cut each rectangle in half diagonally, paying close attention to the direction each is cut. Keep each HRT in its right/left orientation stack. Pair each cut triangle with its corresponding cut triangle, as shown in Figure 2. Refer to Figure 2 to determine the required amount of HRTs. See Half-Rectangle Triangles (p. 16) for HRT piecing and trimming instructions. Trim HRTs to 2.5 in. x 6.5 in. (6.3 cm x 16.5 cm).

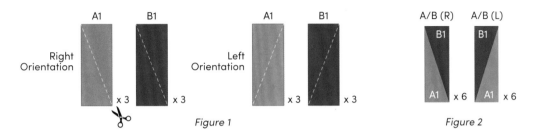

Quilt Assembly

1) To make Block 1, piece together A/B (right) + B2 + B/A (left), as shown in Figure 3. Make two blocks. To make Block 2, piece together B3 + B/A (left), as shown in Figure 4.

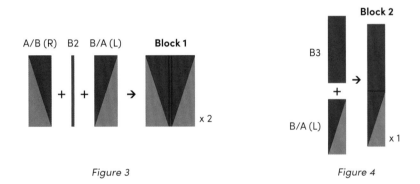

2) To make Block 3, piece together B4 + Block 1, as shown in Figure 5. Make two blocks. To make Block 4, piece together B3 + A/B (right), as shown in Figure 6.

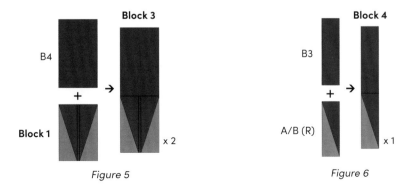

3) To make Block 5, piece together Block 2 + A2 + Block 3 + A2 + Block 3 + A2 + Block 4, as shown in Figure 7.

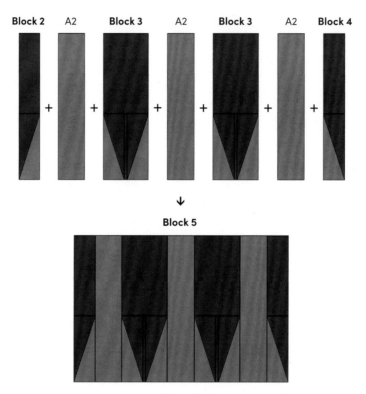

Figure 7

4) To make Block 6, piece together B/A (right) + A3 + A/B (left), as shown in Figure 8. Make three blocks.

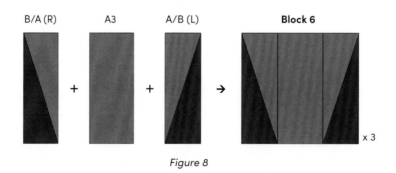

Figure 8

5) From the bottom of each Block 6, cut a 2 in. x 7 in. (5.1 cm x 17.8 cm) strip, as shown in Figure 9. Cut three Bottom Strip blocks. Next, trim .25 in. (.6 cm) off the bottom of each remaining Block 6, as shown in Figure 10.

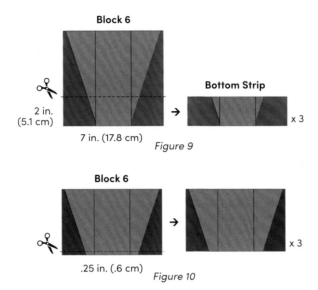

Block 6

2 in.
(5.1 cm)

7 in. (17.8 cm)

Bottom Strip

x 3

Figure 9

Block 6

.25 in. (.6 cm)

x 3

Figure 10

6) From the bottom of each Block 6, cut a 2 in. x 7 in. (5.1 cm x 17.8 cm) strip, as shown in Figure 11. Cut three Middle Strip blocks. From the top of each remaining Block 6, cut a 2 in. x 7 in. (5.1 cm x 17.8 cm) strip, as shown in Figure 12. Cut three Top Strip blocks. Discard remnants.

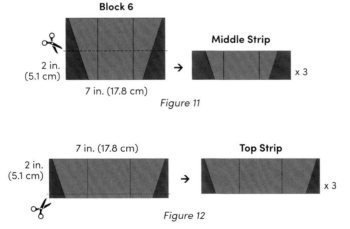

Block 6

2 in.
(5.1 cm)

7 in. (17.8 cm)

Middle Strip

x 3

Figure 11

7 in. (17.8 cm)

2 in.
(5.1 cm)

Top Strip

x 3

Figure 12

7) To make the Bottom Block, piece together Bottom Strip + B5 + Bottom Strip + B5 + Bottom Strip, as shown in Figure 13. To make the Middle Block, piece together Middle Strip + B5 + Middle Strip + B5 + Middle Strip, as shown in Figure 14. To make the Top Block, piece together Top Strip + B5 + Top Strip + B5 + Top Strip, as shown in Figure 15.

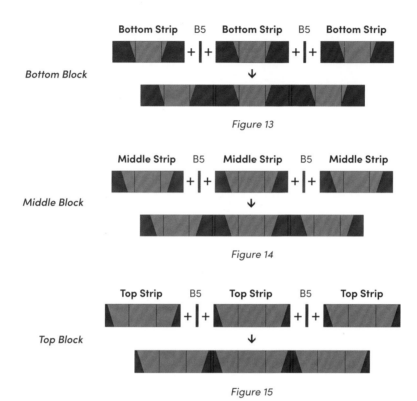

Figure 13

Figure 14

Figure 15

8) To make Block 7, piece together C1 + Top Block + C1 + Middle Block + C1 + Bottom Block, as shown in Figure 16.

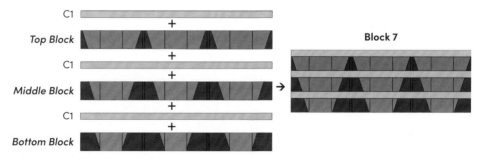

Figure 16

9) Piece together Block 5 + Block 7, as shown in Figure 17.

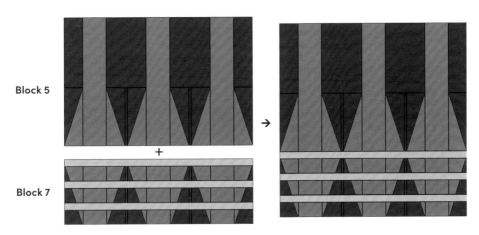

Block 5

Block 7

Figure 17

To finish your Congaree pillow, see Assembling Your Quilt (p. 23)
and Finishing a Pillow Cover (p. 26) or turn this project into a wall hanging (see p. 27).

Congaree Quilt Pattern

Voyageurs
MINNESOTA

With nearly a third of this 218,000-acre park made up of bodies of water, Voyageurs National Park is a network of lakes and streams that surround the Kabetogama Peninsula in northern Minnesota. The peninsula is accessible only by water, and visitors can make a reservation to camp on their own island, rent a houseboat, fish, kayak, explore 100 miles of trails, and in the winter months, snowshoe and cross-country ski. Created using quarter-curves with colors inspired by the aurora borealis, and with half-rectangle triangles to capture one of the more than 500 islands in the park, this wall hanging displays the northern lights, which are best viewed during the fall and winter months.

Finished Measurements | Height: 41 in. (104.1 cm) Width: 35 in. (88.9 cm)

FABRIC: Art Gallery Fabrics *Pure Solids*, 100% cotton
(width: 44 in. [111.75 cm], weight per yard: 4.7 oz)

A (Blueberry Zest) – 1.25 yards

B (Deep Black) – .5 yard

C (Very Berry) – .25 yard

D (Spiceberry) – .25 yard

E (Dark Citron) – .25 yard

F (Fresh Water) – .25 yard

G (Cozumel Blue) – .25 yard

BACKING: Any desired fabric – 2.5 yards

BINDING: Any desired fabric – .33 yard

NOTIONS: Batting – 43 in. x 49 in. (109.2 cm x 124.5 cm)

TEMPLATES: Voyageurs A, Voyageurs B

Cutting Instructions | WALL HANGING

Note: For more information on cutting and assembling blocks, see p. 14.

A (Blueberry Zest)

Cut one 5 in. (12.7 cm) x WOF strip. Subcut:

1 - 5 in. x 6.5 in.
(12.7 cm x 16.5 cm) [A14]

1 - 4 in. x 9.5 in.
(10.2 cm x 24 cm) [A9]

2 - 3.5 in. x 9.5 in.
(8.9 cm x 24 cm) [A10]

Cut two 4 in. (10.2 cm) x WOF strips. Subcut:

10 - Template A

10 - Template B

1 - 3 in. x 10 in.
(7.6 cm x 25.4 cm) [A17]

Cut five 3.5 in. (8.9 cm) x WOF strips. Subcut:

three strips:

12 - 3.5 in. x 9.5 in.
(8.9 cm x 24 cm) [A1]

1 - 3.5 in. x 3.5 in.
(8.9 cm x 8.9 cm) [A2]

one strip:

1 - 3.5 in. x 27 in.
(8.9 cm x 68.6 cm) [A4]

1 - 3.5 in. x 12.5 in.
(8.9 cm x 31.75 cm) [A6]

2 - 1 in. x 3.5 in.
(2.5 cm x 8.9 cm) [A8]

one strip:

1 - 3.5 in. x 22.5 in.
(8.9 cm x 57.1 cm) [A3]

1 - 3.5 in. x 12.5 in.
(8.9 cm x 31.75 cm)
[A6 – 2 total]

1 - 3 in. x 4.5 in.
(7.6 cm x 11.4 cm) [A18]

Cut one 3 in. (7.6 cm) x WOF strip. Subcut:

1 - 3 in. x 41.5 in.
(7.6 cm x 105.4 cm) [A19]

Cut two 2 in. (5.1 cm) x WOF strips. Subcut:

1 - 2 in. x 33 in.
(5.1 cm x 83.8 cm) [A7]

1 - 2 in. x 6.5 in.
(5.1 cm x 16.5 cm) [A5]

1 - 2 in. x 23 in.
(5.1 cm x 58.4 cm) [A12]

1 - 1.5 in. x 15.5 in.
(3.8 cm x 39.4 cm) [A11]

Cut one 2.5 in. (6.3 cm) x WOF strip. Subcut:

1 - 2.5 in. x 21 in.
(6.3 cm x 53.3 cm) [A15]

1 - 2.5 in. x 16.5 in.
(6.3 cm x 42 cm) [A16]

Cut one 1.5 in. (3.8 cm) x WOF strip. Subcut:

2 - 1.5 in. x 16.5 in.
(3.8 cm x 42 cm) [A13]

B (Deep Black)

Cut three 3.5 in. (8.9 cm)
x WOF strips. Subcut:

> **12** – 3.5 in. x 9.5 in.
> (8.9 cm x 24 cm) [B1]
> **1** – 3.5 in. x 3.5 in.
> (8.9 cm x 8.9 cm) [B2]

Cut two 3 in. (7.6 cm)
x WOF strips. Subcut:

> **1** – 3 in. x 21 in.
> (7.6 cm x 53.3 cm) [B3]
> **1** – 3 in. x 26.5 in.
> (7.6 cm x 67.3 cm) [B4]

C (Very Berry)

Cut one 4 in. (10.2 cm)
x WOF strip. Subcut:

> **2** – Template B
> **2** – Template A
> **1** – 3.5 in. x 24 in.
> (8.9 cm x 61 cm) [C1]

D (Spiceberry)

Cut one 4 in. (10.2 cm)
x WOF strip. Subcut:

> **2** – Template B
> **2** – Template A
> **1** – 3.5 in. x 22.5 in.
> (8.9 cm x 57.1 cm) [D1]

E (Dark Citron)

Cut one 4 in. (10.2 cm)
x WOF strip. Subcut:

> **2** – Template B
> **2** – Template A
> **1** – 3.5 in. x 9.5 in.
> (8.9 cm x 24 cm) [E1]

F (Fresh Water)

Cut one 4 in. (10.2 cm)
x WOF strip. Subcut:

> **2** – Template B
> **2** – Template A
> **1** – 3.5 in. x 9.5 in.
> (8.9 cm x 24 cm) [F1]

G (Cozumel Blue)

Cut one 4 in. (10.2 cm)
x WOF strip. Subcut:

> **2** – Template B
> **2** – Template A
> **1** – 3.5 in. x 9.5 in.
> (8.9 cm x 24 cm) [G1]

BINDING *Cut four 2.5 in. (6.3 cm) x WOF strips of the binding fabric.*

Block Assembly

1) This project uses quarter-curve templates (A and B). See Quarter-Curves (p. 15) for quarter-curve piecing and trimming instructions. Refer to Figure 1 to determine the required amount and fabric combinations of the Template Blocks. Trim Template Blocks to 3.5 in. x 3.5 in. (8.9 cm x 8.9 cm).

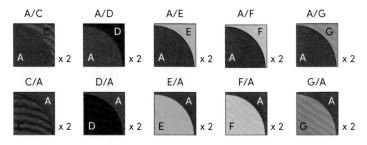

Figure 1

2) HRTs are sewn in two different orientations (right and left). Organize each A1 and B1 rectangle into piles, referring to Figure 2 to determine the required amount for each right/left orientation. Cut each rectangle in half diagonally, paying close attention to the direction each is cut. Keep each HRT in its right/left orientation stack. Pair each cut triangle with its corresponding cut triangle, as shown in Figure 3. Refer to Figure 3 to determine the required amount of HRTs. See Half-Rectangle Triangles (p. 16) for HRT piecing and trimming instructions. Trim HRTs to 2.5 in. x 7.5 in. (6.3 cm x 19 cm).

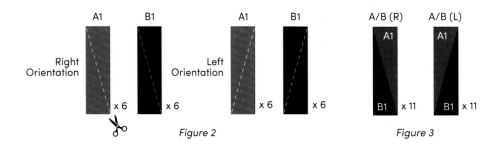

Figure 2   *Figure 3*

3) To make the HSTs, pair A2 and B2, as shown in Figure 4. Refer to Figure 4 to determine the required amount of HSTs. See Half-Square Triangles (p. 19) for two-at-a-time HST piecing and trimming instructions. Trim HSTs to 3 in. x 3 in. (7.6 cm x 7.6 cm).

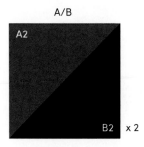

Figure 4

Quilt Assembly

1) To make Block 1, first piece together A/C + A3 + A/D, and D/A + D1 + D/A. Next, piece these rows together, as shown in Figure 5.

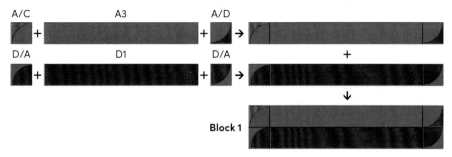

Figure 5

2) To make Block 2, first piece together A4 + A/C; C/A + C1 + C/A; and Block 1 + A5. Then piece these rows together, as shown in Figure 6.

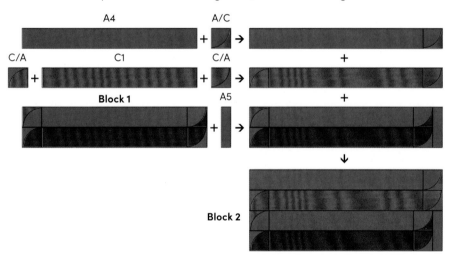

Figure 6

3) To make Block 3, first piece together Block 2 + A6, then piece A7 on top, as shown in Figure 7. To make Block 4, piece together A/D + A8, as shown in Figure 8. To make Block 5, piece together A8 + A/E, as shown in Figure 9.

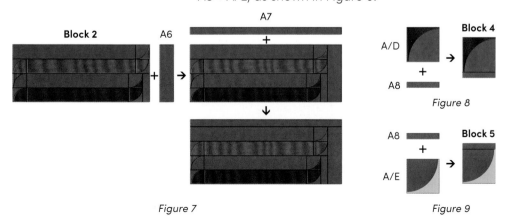

Figure 7

Figure 8

Figure 9

4) To make Block 6, first piece together Block 4 + A9 + Block 5; E/A + E1 + E/A; A/E + A10 + A/F; F/A + F1 + F/A; A/F + A10 + A/G; G/A + G1 + G/A; and A/G + A6. Next, piece these rows together with A11 on the bottom, as shown in Figure 10.

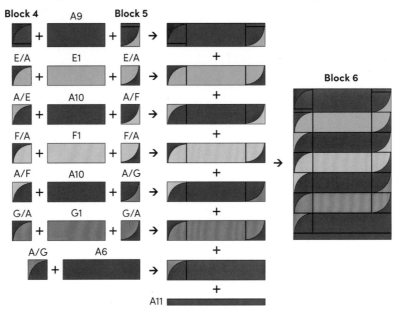

Figure 10

5) To make Block 7, piece together Block 6 + A12, as shown in Figure 11.

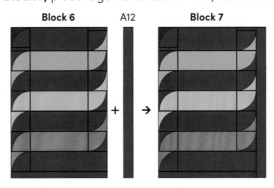

Figure 11

6) To make Block 8, piece together A/B (left) + B/A (right), as shown in Figure 12. Repeat to make eleven blocks. To make Block 9, trim eight Block 8 blocks to 4.5 in. x 5 in. (11.4 cm x 12.7 cm), as shown in Figure 13. Discard piece with the red X.

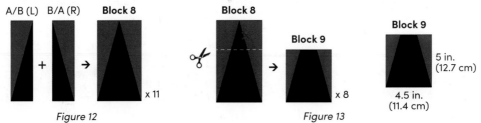

Figure 12   *Figure 13*

7) To make Block 10, piece together Block 8 + Block 9 + Block 9 + Block 9, as shown in Figure 14. Make two. To make Block 11, piece together Block 8 + Block 9 + Block 9, as shown in Figure 15. To make Block 12, first piece together A13 + Block 11 + A13, then piece A14 on top, as shown in Figure 16.

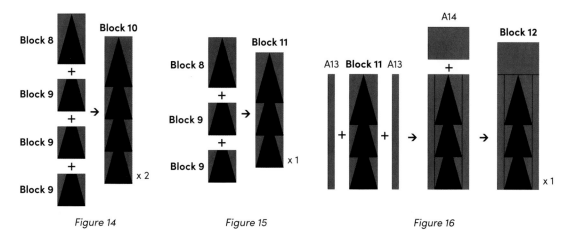

Figure 14   Figure 15   Figure 16

8) To make Block 13, first piece together Block 10 + Block 12 + Block 10 + A15, then piece A16 on top, as shown in Figure 17.

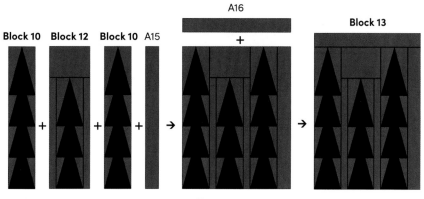

Figure 17

9) To make Block 14, piece together Block 7 + Block 13, as shown in Figure 18.

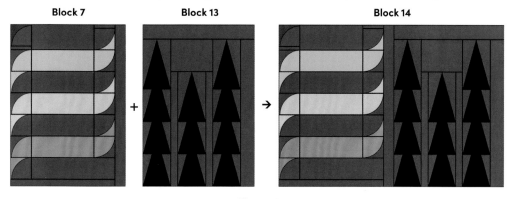

Figure 18

10) To make Block 15, first piece together A17 + A/B + B3, and A18 + A/B + B4. Next, piece these rows together, as shown in Figure 19.

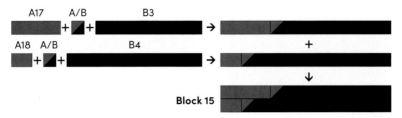

Figure 19

11) To make Block 16, piece together Block 3 + Block 14 + Block 15, as shown in Figure 20.

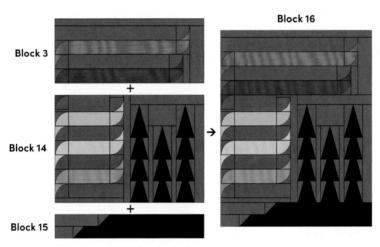

Figure 20

12) Piece together A19 + Block 16, as shown in Figure 21.

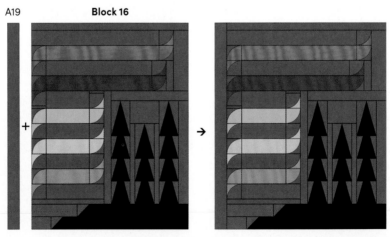

Figure 21

To back and quilt your Voyageurs wall hanging, see Assembling Your Quilt (p. 23); to complete the piece, see Finishing a Wall Hanging (p. 27).

Voyageurs Quilt Pattern

Haleakala

HAWAII

The island of Maui in Hawaii is home to the 30,000-acre Haleakala National Park. Haleakala, which means "house of the sun" in Hawaiian, is known for its spectacular sunrises on Maui's highest peak and dormant volcano. Make sure to book a reservation and pack an extra jacket if you plan to wake up early to view one of these high-altitude, chilly sunrises. Visitors can enjoy hiking, waterfalls, biking, a bamboo forest, and stargazing at Haleakala High Altitude Observatory, one of the best planetariums in the world due to the park's optimal viewing conditions. This wall hanging features fabrics that capture the gorgeous colors of the sun rising above the clouds and uses half-rectangle triangles and half-square triangles for the rugged volcano ridges.

Finished Measurements | Height: 25 in. (63.5 cm) Width: 40 in. (101.6 cm)

FABRIC: Art Gallery Fabrics *Pure Solids*, 100% cotton
(width: 44 in. [111.75 cm], weight per yard: 4.7 oz)

A (Cabernet) – .25 yard

B (Quartz Pink) – .25 yard

C (Candied Cherry) – .25 yard

D (Undeniably Red) – .25 yard

E (Autumnal) – .25 yard

F (Summer Sun) – .25 yard

G (Canary) – .25 yard

H (Honeydew) – .25 yard

BACKING: Any desired fabric – 1.375 yards

BINDING: Any desired fabric – .33 yard

NOTIONS: Batting – 48 in. x 33 in. (122 cm x 83.8 cm)

Cutting Instructions | WALL HANGING

Notes: For more information on cutting and assembling blocks, see p. 14.
Prior to cutting A3, B3, and Fabrics C–H, piece together then measure Row 1.
Cut the remainder of your pieces to match the length of your finished Row 1.

A (Cabernet)

Cut one 3 in. (7.6 cm) x WOF strip. Subcut:

2 - 3 in. x 6 in. (7.6 cm x 15.2 cm) [A1]

6 - 3 in. x 3 in. (7.6 cm x 7.6 cm) [A2]

Cut one 4.5 in. (11.4 cm) x WOF strip. Subcut:

1 - 4.5 in. x 40.5 in. (11.4 cm x 102.9 cm) [A3 – see Notes]

B (Quartz Pink)

Cut one 3 in. (7.6 cm) x WOF strip. Subcut:

2 - 3 in. x 6 in. (7.6 cm x 15.2 cm) [B1]

6 - 3 in. x 3 in. (7.6 cm x 7.6 cm) [B2]

Cut one 1.5 in. (3.8 cm) x WOF strip. Subcut:

1 - 1.5 in. x 40.5 in. (3.8 cm x 102.9 cm) [B3 – see Notes]

C (Candied Cherry)

Cut one 3.5 in. (8.9 cm) x WOF strip. Subcut:

1 - 3.5 in. x 40.5 in. (8.9 cm x 102.9 cm) [C1 – see Notes]

D (Undeniably Red)

Cut one 3.5 in. (8.9 cm) x WOF strip. Subcut:

1 - 3.5 in. x 40.5 in. (8.9 cm x 102.9 cm) [D1 – see Notes]

E (Autumnal)

Cut one 3.5 in. (8.9 cm) x WOF strip. Subcut:

1 - 3.5 in. x 40.5 in. (8.9 cm x 102.9 cm) [E1 – see Notes]

F (Summer Sun)

Cut one 3.5 in. (8.9 cm) x WOF strip. Subcut:

1 - 3.5 in. x 40.5 in. (8.9 cm x 102.9 cm) [F1 – see Notes]

G (Canary)

Cut one 3.5 in. (8.9 cm) x WOF strip. Subcut:

1 - 3.5 in. x 40.5 in. (8.9 cm x 102.9 cm) [G1 – see Notes]

H (Honeydew)

Cut one 3.5 in. (8.9 cm) x WOF strip. Subcut:

1 - 3.5 in. x 40.5 in. (8.9 cm x 102.9 cm) [H1 – see Notes]

BINDING *Cut four 2.5 in. (6.3 cm) x WOF strips of the binding fabric.*

Block Assembly

1) To make the HSTs, pair A2 and B2, as shown in Figure 1. Refer to Figure 1 to determine the required amount of HSTs. See Half-Square Triangles (p. 19) for two-at-a-time HST piecing and trimming instructions. Trim HSTs to 2.5 in. x 2.5 in. (6.3 cm x 6.3 cm).

Figure 1

2) HRTs are sewn in two different orientations (right and left). Organize each A1 and B1 rectangle into piles, referring to Figure 2 to determine the required amount for each right/left orientation. Cut each rectangle in half diagonally, paying close attention to the direction each is cut. Keep each HRT in its right/left orientation stack. Pair each cut triangle with its corresponding cut triangle, as shown in Figure 3. Refer to Figure 3 to determine the required amount of HRTs. See Half-Rectangle Triangles (p. 16) for HRT piecing and trimming instructions. Trim HRTs to 2.5 in. x 4.5 in. (6.3 cm x 11.4 cm).

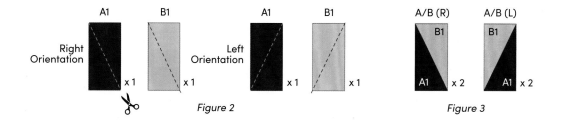

Figure 2   *Figure 3*

Quilt Assembly

1) To make Row 1, piece blocks together in the order shown in Figure 4.

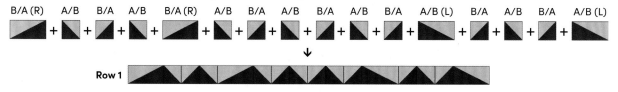

Figure 4

2) Piece together H1 + G1 + F1 + E1 + D1 + C1 + B3 + Row 1 + A3, as shown in Figure 5.

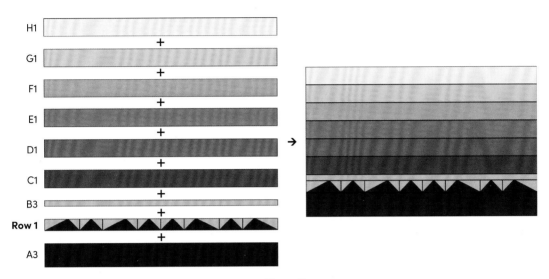

Figure 5

To back and quilt your Haleakala wall hanging, see Assembling Your Quilt (p. 23); to complete your piece, see Finishing a Wall Hanging (p. 27).

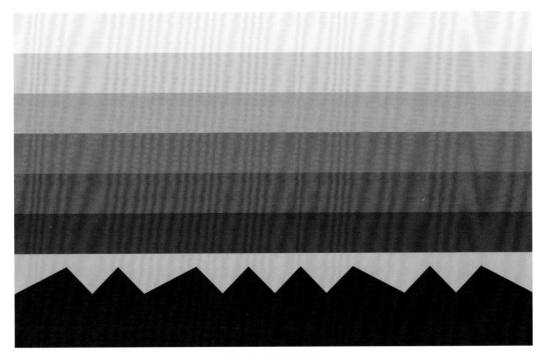

Haleakala Quilt Pattern

New River Gorge

WEST VIRGINIA

One of the oldest rivers in the world, the New River in West Virginia flows south to north and has carved the deepest gorge in the Appalachian Mountains. New River Gorge National Park sits on 73,000 acres along 53 miles of the river, and is home to the thirteenth-highest bridge in the world, which was built 876 feet above the river. For a unique experience, you can book a tour to walk on a catwalk located 25 feet below the bridge. On Bridge Day, an annual event that closes the bridge to traffic, you can walk across, BASE jump, rappel, or take a zip line from the longest single-span steel arch bridge in the country. The park is known for some of the country's best whitewater rafting, but you can also enjoy rock climbing, fishing, hiking, and biking. This wall hanging uses quarter-curves to recreate the river gorge in vibrant fall foliage with rich yellow, umber, and orange fabrics.

Finished Measurements | Height: 36 in. (91.4 cm) Width: 30 in. (76.2 cm)

FABRIC: Art Gallery Fabrics *Pure Solids*, 100% cotton
(width: 44 in. [111.75 cm], weight per yard: 4.7 oz)

■ **A** (Teak) – .5 yard

□ **B** (Morning Frost) – .33 yard

■ **C** (Lemon Tart) – .625 yard

■ **D** (Apple Cider) – .25 yard

BACKING: Any desired fabric – 1.25 yards

BINDING: Any desired fabric – .33 yard

NOTIONS: Batting – 38 in. x 44 in. (96.5 cm x 111.7 cm)

TEMPLATES: New River Gorge/Grand Canyon 1A, New River Gorge/Grand Canyon 1B, New River Gorge 2A, New River Gorge 2B

Cutting Instructions | WALL HANGING

Note: For more information on cutting and assembling blocks, see p. 14.

■ A (Teak)

Cut one 5 in. (12.7 cm) x WOF strip. Subcut:

- **5** – Template 1B
- **3** – Template 1A
- **1** – 4.5 in. x 12.5 in. (11.4 cm x 31.75 cm) [A5]

Cut one 9 in. (22.9 cm) x WOF strip. Subcut:

- **2** – Template 2A
- **1** – 4.5 in. x 11 in. (11.4 cm x 28 cm) [A1]
- **1** – 4.5 in. x 15 in. (11.4 cm x 38 cm) [A2]
- **1** – 4.5 in. x 16.5 in. (11.4 cm x 42 cm) [A6]
- **1** – 4.5 in. x 4.5 in. (11.4 cm x 11.4 cm) [A4]

Cut one 2.5 in. (6.3 cm) x WOF strip. Subcut:

- **1** – 2.5 in. x 27 in. (6.3 cm x 68.6 cm) [A3]

□ B (Morning Frost)

Cut one 8.5 in. (21.6 cm) x WOF strip. Subcut:

- **1** – 8.5 in. x 8.5 in. (21.6 cm x 21.6 cm) [B2]
- **2** – 4.5 in. x 4.5 in. (11.4 cm x 11.4 cm) [B1]
- **3** – Template 1B
- **3** – Template 1A

■ C (Lemon Tart)

Cut one 10 in. (25.4 cm) x WOF strip. Subcut:

- **1** – 10 in. x 10.5 in. (25.4 cm x 26.7 cm) [C1]
- **2** – Template 2B
- **4** – Template 1B
- **2** – Template 1A

Cut one 9.5 in. (24 cm) x WOF strip. Subcut:

- **1** – 9.5 in. x 12.5 in. (24 cm x 31.75 cm) [C5]
- **1** – 8.5 in. x 12.5 in. (21.6 cm x 31.75 cm) [C6]

- **1** – 3.5 in. x 8.5 in. (8.9 cm x 12.6 cm) [C2]
- **1** – 4.5 in. x 11.5 in. (11.4 cm x 29.2 cm) [C3]
- **1** – 4.5 in. x 4.5 in. (11.4 cm x 11.4 cm) [C4]

■ D (Apple Cider)

Cut one 5 in. (12.7 cm) x WOF strip. Subcut:

- **4** – Template 1A

BINDING *Cut four 2.5 in. (6.3 cm) x WOF strips of the binding fabric.*

Block Assembly

1) This project uses quarter-curve templates (1A, 1B, 2A, and 2B). See Quarter-Curves (p. 15) for quarter-curve piecing and trimming instructions. Refer to Figure 1 to determine the required amount and fabric combinations of Template Blocks. Trim Template Block 1 to 4.5 in. x 4.5 in. (11.4 cm x 11.4 cm) and Template Block 2 to 8.5 in. x 8.5 in. (21.6 cm x 21.6 cm).

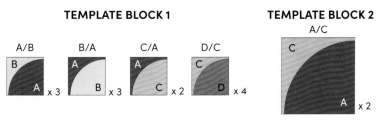

Figure 1

Quilt Assembly

1) To make Block 1, piece together A1 + B/A, as shown in Figure 2. To make Block 2, first piece together A2 + Block 1, and A/B + B1, then piece these units together with A/C (Template Block 2) on top, as shown in Figure 3. To make Block 3, piece together A3 + Block 2, as shown in Figure 4.

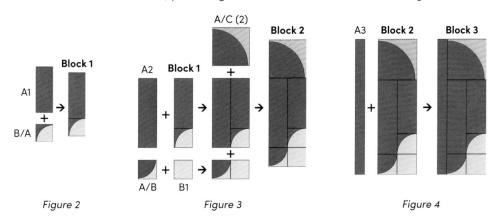

Figure 2   *Figure 3*   *Figure 4*

2) To make Block 4, piece together C1 + Block 3, as shown in Figure 5. To make Block 5, piece together D/C + D/C, and D/C + D/C. Next, piece these rows together with C2 on top, as shown in Figure 6. To make Block 6, piece together A/B + B1, as shown in Figure 7.

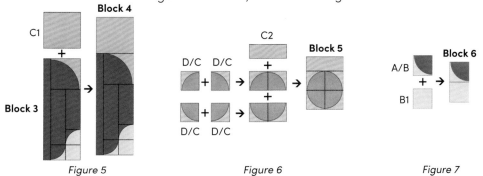

Figure 5   *Figure 6*   *Figure 7*

3) To make Block 7, piece together C3 + Block 5; C/A (Template Block 1) + C4 + C/A (Template Block 1); A/B + B/A + A4; and B2 + Block 6. Next, piece these rows together with C5 in the order shown in Figure 8. To make Block 8, piece together A5 + B/A, then piece A6 to the right of this block. Next, piece this block together with C6 and C/A (Template Block 2), as shown in Figure 9.

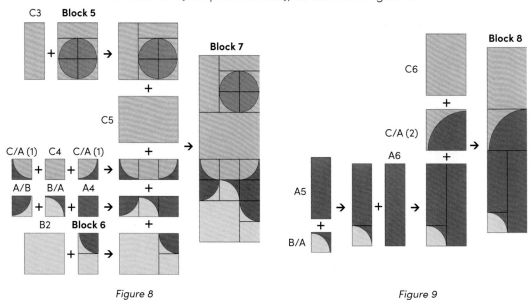

Figure 8   Figure 9

4) Piece together Block 4 + Block 7 + Block 8, as shown in Figure 10.

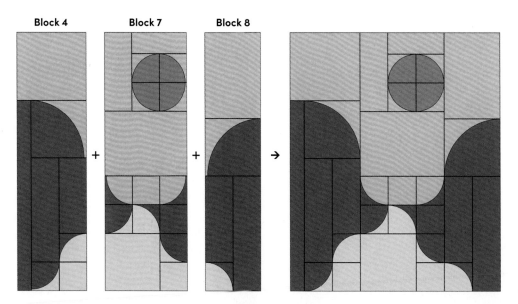

Figure 10

To back and quilt your New River Gorge wall hanging, see Assembling Your Quilt (p. 23); to complete the piece, see Finishing a Wall Hanging (p. 27).

New River Gorge Quilt Pattern

Indiana Dunes

INDIANA

Indiana Dunes National Park, located along 15 miles of Lake Michigan shoreline, is known for its dunes that tower nearly 200 feet above the lake. The dunes are home to more than 1,100 plant species and ferns, and more than 350 bird species have been observed at the park. Birders enjoy the Big May Day Bird Count during the annual Birding Festival, where teams attempt to spot as many bird species as possible within twenty-four hours. Other activities include swimming, hiking, camping, and fishing, plus skiing and snowshoeing during the winter. This wall hanging captures the layers of the beach from vegetation to shoreline, to the lake meeting the skyline in the distance, using half-rectangle triangles in soft beach tones.

Finished Measurements | Height: 30 in. (76.2 cm) Width: 30 in. (76.2 cm)

FABRIC: Art Gallery Fabrics *Pure Solids*, 100% cotton
(width: 44 in. [111.75 cm], weight per yard: 4.7 oz)

A (Vaporous) – .25 yard

B (Morning Frost) – .5 yard

C (Swimming Pool) – .25 yard

D (Latte) – .25 yard

E (Macchiato) – .25 yard

F (Coconut Milk) – .25 yard

G (Fresh Aloe) – .25 yard

BACKING: Any desired fabric – 1.25 yards

BINDING: Any desired fabric – .33 yard

NOTIONS: Batting – 38 in. x 38 in. (96.5 cm x 96.5 cm)

Cutting Instructions | WALL HANGING

Note: For more information on cutting and assembling blocks, see p. 14.

A (Vaporous)

Cut one 3.5 in. (8.9 cm) x WOF strip. Subcut:

1 – 3.5 in. x 30.5 in. (8.9 cm x 77.5 cm) [A1]

B (Morning Frost)

Cut one 9.5 in. (24 cm) x WOF strip. Subcut:

1 – 9.5 in. x 30.5 in. (24 cm x 77.5 cm) [B6]

1 – 3.75 in. x 8.25 in. (9.5 cm x 21 cm) [B1]

Cut one 3.75 in. (9.5 cm) x WOF strip. Subcut:

2 – 3.75 in. x 8.25 in. (9.5 cm x 21 cm) [B1 – 3 total]

1 – 2.75 in. x 18.5 in. (7 cm x 47 cm) [B3]

1 – 2.75 in. x 6.5 in. (7 cm x 16.5 cm) [B5]

Cut one 2.75 in. (7 cm) x WOF strip. Subcut:

1 – 2.75 in. x 24.5 in. (7 cm x 62.2 cm) [B2]

1 – 2.75 in. x 12.5 in. (7 cm x 31.7 cm) [B4]

C (Swimming Pool)

Cut one 3.75 in. (9.5 cm) x WOF strip. Subcut:

5 – 3.75 in. x 8.25 in. (9.5 cm x 21 cm) [C1]

D (Latte)

Cut two 3.75 in. (9.5 cm) x WOF strips. Subcut:

10 – 3.75 in. x 8.25 in. (9.5 cm x 21 cm) [D1]

E (Macchiato)

Cut one 3.75 in. (9.5 cm) x WOF strip. Subcut:

5 – 3.75 in. x 8.25 in. (9.5 cm x 21 cm) [E1]

F (Coconut Milk)

Cut one 3.75 in. (9.5 cm) x WOF strip. Subcut:

5 – 3.75 in. x 8.25 in. (9.5 cm x 21 cm) [F1]

G (Fresh Aloe)

Cut one 3.75 in. (9.5 cm) x WOF strip. Subcut:

3 – 3.75 in. x 8.25 in. (9.5 cm x 21 cm) [G1]

BINDING *Cut four 2.5 in. (6.3 cm) x WOF strips of the binding fabric.*

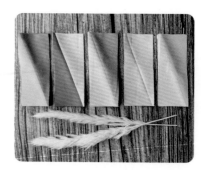

Block Assembly

1) For this wall hanging, HRTs are sewn in one orientation (right). Cut each B1, C1, D1, E1, F1, and G1 rectangle in half diagonally, paying close attention to the direction each is cut (see Figure 1). Pair each cut triangle with its cut corresponding triangle, as shown in Figure 2. Refer to Figure 2 to determine the required amount and fabric combinations of the HRTs. See Half-Rectangle Triangles (p. 16) for HRT piecing and trimming instructions. Trim HRTs to 2.75 in. x 6.5 in. (7 cm x 16.5 cm).

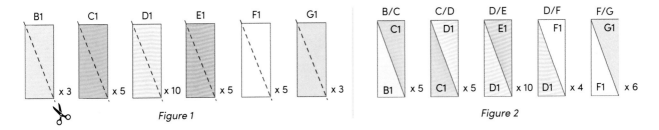

Figure 1

Figure 2

Quilt Assembly

1) To make Rows 1–8, piece blocks together in the order shown in Figure 3.

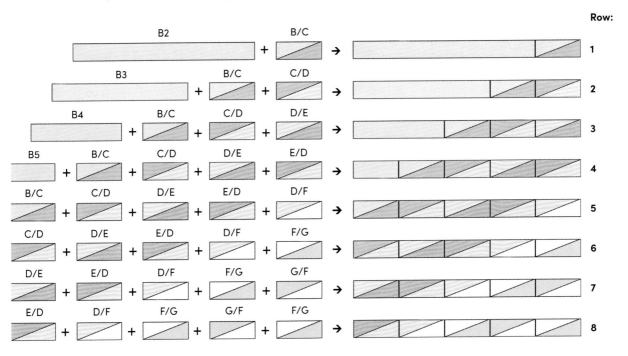

Figure 3

2) Piece together A1 + B6 + Rows 1–8, as shown in Figure 4.

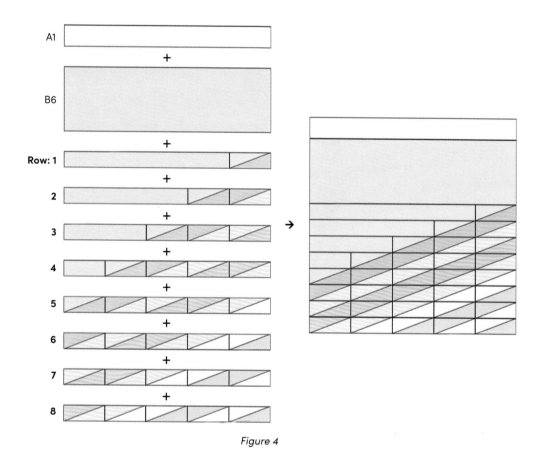

Figure 4

To back and quilt your Indiana Dunes wall hanging, see Assembling Your Quilt (p. 23); to complete the piece, see Finishing a Wall Hanging (p. 27).

Indiana Dunes Quilt Pattern

Quilts

Yosemite

CALIFORNIA

S panning 747,000 acres within California's Sierra Nevada Mountains, Yosemite National Park is known for its lakes, mountains, granite cliffs, giant sequoia trees, glaciers, and waterfalls. Yosemite is home to more than twenty-five waterfalls, including Yosemite Falls, which, at 2,425 feet, is the tallest in North America. For a unique waterfall experience, during the second week of February check out another one of the park's waterfalls, Horsetail Falls. If the falls are flowing and the sky is clear, Horsetail Falls will be illuminated by the setting sun to create a fiery, molten lava red-orange glow known as Firefall. With cool mountain blues and a pop of gold, this baby quilt offers a playful splash using curves and half-rectangle triangles to create the cascading Yosemite Falls.

Finished Measurements | Height: 40 in. (101.6 cm) Width: 36 in. (91.4 cm)

FABRIC: Art Gallery Fabrics *Pure Solids*, 100% cotton
(width: 44 in. [111.75 cm], weight per yard: 4.7 oz)

A (Heart of the Ocean) – .875 yard

B (Aero Blue) – .375 yard

C (Tranquil Waters) – .625 yard

D (Raw Gold) – .25 yard

BACKING: Any desired
fabric – 2.5 yards

BINDING: Any desired
fabric – .33 yard

NOTIONS: Batting – 44 in.
x 48 in. (111.7 cm x 122 cm

TEMPLATES: Yosemite 1A,
Yosemite 1B, Yosemite 2A,
Yosemite 2B

Cutting Instructions | BABY QUILT

Notes: Template Block 2 has right and left orientation curves. Flip Template 2A and 2B over
to cut (1) right orientation piece. For more information on cutting and assembling blocks, see p. 14.

■ A (Heart of the Ocean)

*Cut one 15.5 in. (39.4 cm)
x WOF strip. Subcut:*

1 – 15.5 in. x 16.5 in.
(39.4 cm x 42 cm) [A7]

1 – 10.5 in. x 15.5 in.
(26.7 cm x 39.4 cm) [A6]

1 – 9 in. x 14 in.
(22.9 cm x 35.5 cm) [A9]

1 – 3 in. x 8.5 in.
(7.6 cm x 21.6 cm) [A3]

1 – 2.5 in. x 3 in.
(6.3 cm x 7.6 cm) [A2]

*Cut one 8 in. (20.3 cm)
x WOF strip. Subcut:*

1 – 8 in. x 9 in.
(20.3 cm x 22.9 cm) [A8]

2 – 3 in. x 8 in.
(7.6 cm x 20.3 cm) [A5]

4 – 4 in. x 10 in.
(10.2 cm x 25.4 cm) [A1]

1 – 5.5 in. x 7 in.
(14 cm x 17.8 cm) [A4]

*Cut one 3.5 in. (8.9 cm)
x WOF strip. Subcut:*

5 - Template 2A (see Notes)

*Cut two 1.5 in. (3.8 cm)
x WOF strips. Subcut:*

1 – 1.5 in. x 7.5 in.
(3.8 cm x 19 cm) [A10]

1 – 1.5 in. x 13.5 in.
(3.8 cm x 34.3 cm) [A11]

1 – 1.5 in. x 7 in.
(3.8 cm x 17.8 cm) [A12]

1 – 1.5 in. x 13 in.
(3.8 cm x 33 cm) [A13]

1 – 1.5 in. x 6.5 in.
(3.8 cm x 16.5 cm) [A14]

1 – 1.5 in. x 12.5 in.
(3.8 cm x 31.7 cm) [A15]

1 – 1.5 in. x 6 in.
(3.8 cm x 15.2 cm) [A16]

1 – 1.5 in. x 12 in.
(3.8 cm x 30.5 cm) [A17]

■ B (Aero Blue)

*Cut one 6 in. (15.2 cm)
x WOF strip. Subcut:*

1 - Template 1B

1 – 5.5 in. x 8 in.
(14 cm x 20.3 cm) [B2]

1 – 3 in. x 10.5 in.
(7.6 cm x 26.7 cm) [B3]

1 – 1.5 in. x 15.5 in.
(3.8 cm x 39.4 cm) [B4]

*Cut one 4 in. (10.2 cm)
x WOF strip. Subcut:*

4 – 4 in. x 10 in.
(10.2 cm x 25.4 cm) [B1]

*Cut one 1.5 in. (3.8 cm)
x WOF strip. Subcut:*

1 – 1.5 in. x 17.5 in.
(3.8 cm x 44.4 cm) [B5]

1 – 1.5 in. x 19.5 in.
(3.8 cm x 49.5 cm) [B6]

C (Tranquil Waters)

Cut one 8 in. (20.3 cm) x WOF strip. Subcut:

1 - 8 in. x 16 in. (20.3 cm x 40.6 cm) [C4]

1 - 4.5 in. x 8 in. (11.4 cm x 20.3 cm) [C3]

1 - 3 in. x 10.5 in. (7.6 cm x 26.7 cm) [C1]

1 - Template 1A

Cut one 3.5 in. (8.9 cm) x WOF strip. Subcut:

5 - Template 2B (see Notes)

Cut one 6 in. (15.2 cm) x WOF strip. Subcut:

1 - Template 1B

1 - 5.5 in. x 7 in. (14 cm x 17.8 cm) [C2]

1 - 3 in. x 23.5 in. (7.6 cm x 59.7 cm) [C5]

1 - 1.5 in. x 16.5 in. (3.8 cm x 42 cm) [C6]

1 - 1.5 in. x 18.5 in. (3.8 cm x 47 cm) [C7]

D (Raw Gold)

Cut one 5.5 in. (14 cm) x WOF strip. Subcut:

1 - Template 1A

BINDING *Cut four 2.5 in. (6.3 cm) x WOF strips of the binding fabric.*

Block Assembly

1) The Yosemite National Park quilt uses half- and quarter-curve templates (1A, 1B, 2A, and 2B). See Half-Curves (p. 14) and Quarter-Curves (p. 15) for half- and quarter-curve piecing and trimming instructions. Refer to Figure 1 to determine the required amount and fabric combinations of the Template Blocks. Note: Template Block 2 has left and right orientation curves. Trim Template Block 1 to 5.5 in. x 10.5 in. (14 cm x 26.7 cm), and Template Block 2 to 3 in. x 7 in. (7.6 cm x 17.8 cm).

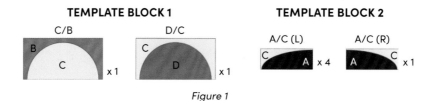

Figure 1

2) HRTs are sewn in two different orientations (right and left). Organize each A1 and B1 rectangle into piles, referring to Figure 2 to determine the required amount of each right/left orientation. Cut each rectangle in half diagonally, paying close attention to the direction each is cut. Keep each HRT in its right/left orientation stack. Pair each cut triangle with its corresponding cut triangle, as shown in Figure 3. Refer to Figure 3 to determine the required amount of HRTs. See Half-Rectangle Triangles (p. 16) for HRT piecing and trimming instructions. Trim HRTs to 3 in. x 8 in. (7.6 cm x 20.3 cm).

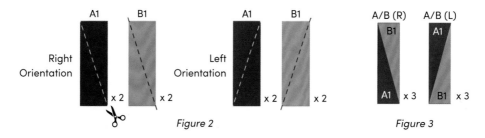

Figure 2   *Figure 3*

Quilt Assembly

1) To make Row 1, first piece together D/C + C1, then C2 + A/C (left), then piece these blocks together with C3 and C4, as shown in Figure 4.

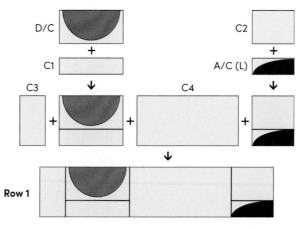

Figure 4

2) To make Block 1, first piece together C5 + A/C (left), and A/C (left) + A2 + A/C (right) + A/C (left) + A3. Next, piece these rows together, as shown in Figure 5.

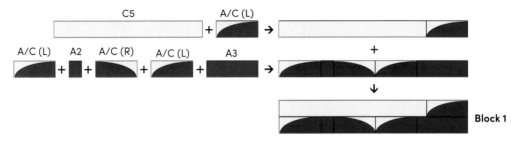

Figure 5

3) To make Row 2, piece together Block 1 + A4, as shown in Figure 6.

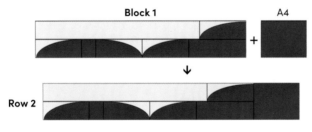

Figure 6

4) To make Block 2, first piece together A5 + A/B (left) + B/A (right) + A5, and A/B (left) + B2 + B/A (right). Next, piece these rows together, as shown in Figure 7.

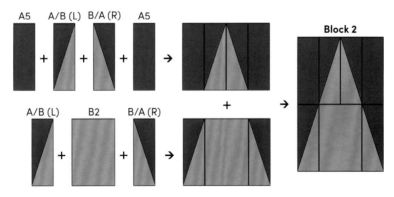

Figure 7

5) To make Row 3, piece together A6 + Block 2 + A7, as shown in Figure 8.

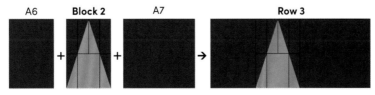

Figure 8

6) To make Block 3, piece together B3 + C/B, as shown in Figure 9.

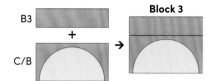

Figure 9

7) To make Block 4, first piece together A/B (left) + Block 3 + B/A (right), then piece B4 to the bottom, as shown in Figure 10.

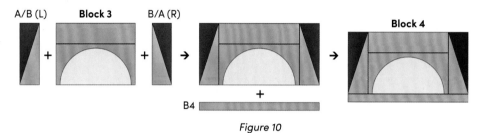

Figure 10

8) To make Row 4, piece together A8 + Block 4 + A9, as shown in Figure 11.

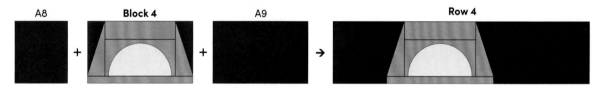

Figure 11

9) To make Row 5, first piece together A10 + C6 + A11; A12 + B5 + A13; A14 + C7 + A15; and A16 + B6 + A17. Next, piece these rows together, as shown in Figure 12.

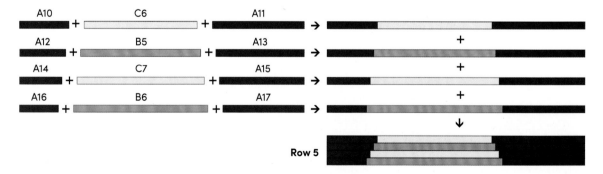

Figure 12

10) Piece together Rows 1–5, as shown in Figure 13.

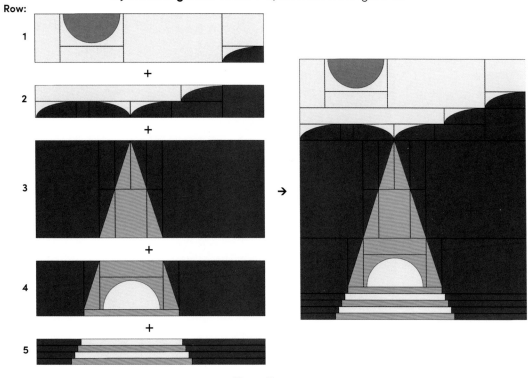

Figure 13

To back and quilt your Yosemite baby quilt, see Assembling Your Quilt (p. 23).

Yosemite Quilt Pattern

Rocky Mountain

COLORADO

Located in northern Colorado on 265,000 acres, Rocky Mountain National Park has 147 alpine lakes and 77 towering mountain peaks with heights of more than 12,000 feet. There are also more than 1,000 types of wildflowers and 141 species of butterflies that you can see while hiking the more than 300 miles of trails through meadows, wilderness, and alpine regions of the park. For a more laid-back activity, there is the scenic drive along the 48-mile Trail Ridge Road, known as the "highway to the sky." This drive provides panoramic views of the Rocky Mountains with a peak elevation of more than 12,000 feet. Though one-third of the park is above the tree line, this baby quilt uses half-rectangle triangles and half-square triangles in soft-hued alpine forest colors to create a scene of soaring pines with a gentle mountain range in the distance.

Finished Measurements | Height: 44 in. (111.75 cm) Width: 44 in. (111.75 cm)

FABRIC: Art Gallery Fabrics *Pure Solids*, 100% cotton
(width: 44 in. [111.75 cm], weight per yard: 4.7 oz)

■ **A** (Asparagus) – .5 yard

■ **B** (Lava Rock) – .625 yard

□ **C** (Crystalline) – 1.33 yards

BACKING: Any desired fabric – 3 yards

BINDING: Any desired fabric – .5 yard

NOTIONS: Batting – 52 in. x 52 in. (132 cm x 132 cm)

Cutting Instructions | BABY QUILT

Note: For more information on cutting and assembling blocks, see p. 14.

■ **A** (Asparagus)

Cut one 7.5 in. (19 cm) x WOF strip. Subcut:

10 – 3.75 in. x 7.5 in.
(9.5 cm x 19 cm) [A1]

Cut two 3.75 in. (9.5 cm) x WOF strips. Subcut:

17 – 3.75 in. x 3.75 in.
(9.5 cm x 9.5 cm) [A2]

2 – 3.25 in. x 3.25 in.
(8.2 cm x 8.2 cm) [A3]

3 – 1.25 in. x 1.75 in.
(3.2 cm x 4.4 cm) [A4]

■ **B** (Lava Rock)

Cut one 7.5 in. (19 cm) x WOF strip. Subcut:

4 – 3.75 in. x 7.5 in.
(9.5 cm x 19 cm) [B1]

9 – 3.75 in. x 3.75 in.
(9.5 cm x 9.5 cm) [B3]

1 – 3.25 in. x 6.5 in.
(8.2 cm x 16.5 cm) [B8]

1 – 3.25 in. x 5.5 in.
(8.2 cm x 14 cm) [B9]

2 – 2 in. x 3.25 in.
(5.1 cm x 8.2 cm) [B7]

Cut one 4.75 in. (12 cm) x WOF strip. Subcut:

2 – 4.75 in. x 9.5 in.
(12 cm x 24 cm) [B2]

1 – 3.25 in. x 6 in.
(8.2 cm x 15.2 cm) [B4]

3 – 3.25 in. x 3.25 in.
(8.2 cm x 8.2 cm) [B5]

2 – 1.75 in. x 3.25 in.
(4.4 cm x 8.2 cm) [B6]

1 – 1.25 in. x 1.75 in.
(3.2 cm x 4.4 cm) [B10]

1 – 1.75 in. x 1.75 in.
(4.4 cm x 4.4 cm) [B11]

1 – 1.75 in. x 2.5 in.
(4.4 cm x 6.3 cm) [B12]

Cut one 4.5 in. (11.4 cm) x WOF strip. Subcut:

1 – 4.5 in. x 10.5 in.
(11.4 cm x 26.7 cm) [B15]

1 – 4.5 in. x 9.75 in.
(11.4 cm x 24.7 cm) [B16]

1 – 4.5 in. x 6.5 in.
(11.4 cm x 16.5 cm) [B17]

1 – 4.5 in. x 11 in.
(11.4 cm x 28 cm) [B18]

1 – 1.75 in. x 2 in.
(4.4 cm x 5.1 cm) [B13]

1 – 1 in. x 1.75 in.
(2.5 cm x 4.4 cm) [B14]

□ **C** (Crystalline)

Cut two 7.5 in. (19 cm) x WOF strips. Sew together, then subcut:

1 – 7.5 in. x 44.5 in.
(19 cm x 113 cm) [C21]

8 – 3.75 in. x 7.5 in.
(9.5 cm x 19 cm) [C1]

3 – 3.75 in. x 3.75 in.
(9.5 cm x 9.5 cm) [C3]

Cut one 3.75 in. (9.5 cm) x WOF strip. Subcut:

11 – 3.75 in. x 3.75 in.
(9.5 cm x 9.5 cm)
[C3 – 14 total]

*Cut one 4.75 in. (12 cm)
x WOF strip. Subcut:*

    2 – 4.75 in. x 9.5 in.
(12 cm x 24 cm) [C2]

    2 – 3.25 in. x 5.25 in.
(8.2 cm x 13.3 cm) [C17]

*Cut seven 3.25 in. (8.2 cm)
x WOF strips. Subcut:*

one strip:

    1 – 3.25 in. x 21.5 in.
(8.2 cm x 54.6 cm) [C5]

    1 – 3.25 in. x 20.5 in.
(8.2 cm x 52.1 cm) [C7]

one strip:

    2 – 3.25 in. x 17 in.
(8.2 cm x 43.2 cm) [C8]

    1 – 3.25 in. x 7.75 in.
(8.2 cm x 19.7 cm) [C11]

one strip:

    7 – 3.25 in. x 6 in.
(8.2 cm x 15.2 cm) [C9]

one strip:

    1 – 3.25 in. x 11.5 in.
(8.2 cm x 29.2 cm) [C10]

    4 – 3.25 in. x 3.25 in.
(8.2 cm x 8.2 cm) [C14]

    1 – 3.25 in. x 7.75 in.
(8.2 cm x 19.7 cm) [C18]

    1 – 3.25 in. x 7.5 in.
(8.2 cm x 19 cm) [C20]

one strip:

    1 – 3.25 in. x 21.75 in.
(8.2 cm x 55.2 cm) [C6]

    1 – 3.25 in. x 19.75 in.
(8.2 cm x 50.1 cm) [C13]

one strip:

    1 – 3.25 in. x 20.75 in.
(8.2 cm x 52. 7 cm) [C4]

    1 – 3.25 in. x 9.75 in.
(8.2 cm x 24.7 cm) [C12]

    1 – 3.25 in. x 9.5 in.
(8.2 cm x 24 cm) [C16]

one strip:

    4 – 3.25 in. x 8.75 in.
(8.2 cm x 22.2 cm) [C15]

    1 – 3.25 in. x 3.5 in.
(8.2 cm x 8.9 cm) [C19]

BINDING *Cut five 2.5 in.
(6.3 cm) x WOF strips of the
binding fabric.*

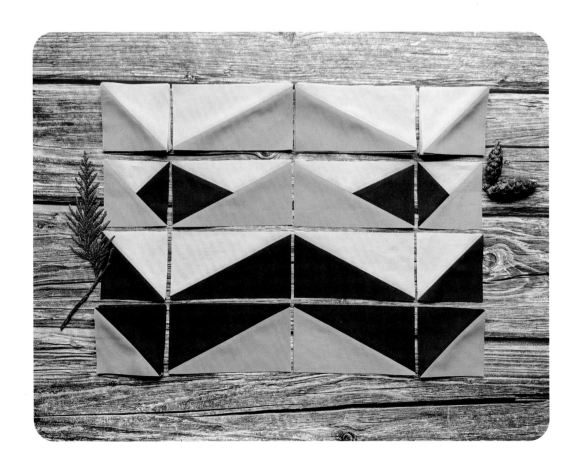

Block Assembly

1) HRTs are sewn in two different orientations (right and left). Organize each A1, B1, C1, B2, and C2 rectangle into piles, referring to Figure 1 to determine the required amount for each right/left orientation. Cut each rectangle in half diagonally, paying close attention to the direction each is cut. Keep each HRT in its right/left orientation stack.

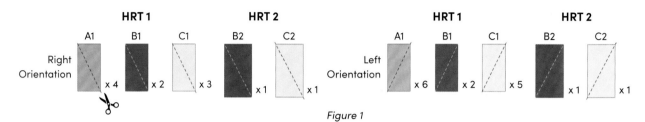

Figure 1

2) Pair each cut triangle with its corresponding cut triangle, as shown in Figure 2. Refer to Figure 2 to determine the required amount and fabric combinations of the HRTs. See Half-Rectangle Triangles (p. 16) for HRT piecing and trimming instructions. Trim HRT 1 to 3.25 in. x 6 in. (8.2 cm x 15.2 cm) and HRT 2 to 3.75 in. x 7.5 in. (9.5 cm x 19 cm).

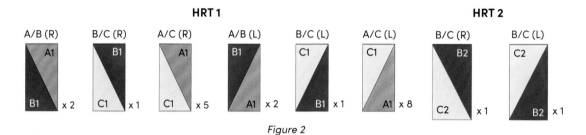

Figure 2

3) To make HRT 3, cut each trimmed HRT 2 block in half on the diagonal for each orientation, as shown in Figure 3. Discard the triangle with the red X and align each HRT 2 triangle with the remaining A1 triangles. Make one HRT 3 (left) and one HRT 3 (right). Trim HRT 3 to 3.25 in. x 6 in. (8.2 cm x 15.2 cm).

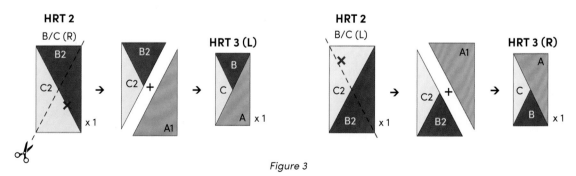

Figure 3

4) To make the HSTs, pair each A2, B3, and C3 square with its corresponding square, as shown in Figure 4. Refer to Figure 4 to determine the required amount and fabric combinations of HSTs. See Half-Square Triangles (p. 19) for two-at-a-time HST piecing and trimming instructions. Trim HSTs to 3.25 in. x 3.25 in. (8.2 cm x 8.2 cm).

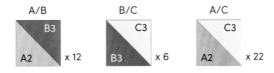

Figure 4

5) After trimming the HSTs, take two B/C HSTs and pair each with an A3 square. Place A3 on top of a B/C HST and draw a diagonal line through the block, perpendicular to the B/C seam, as shown in Figure 5. Sew directly on the marked center line. Trim a .25 in. (.6 cm) seam allowance on the dotted line toward the side of the HST with the red X and press the seams open. Discard the trimmed piece. Make two HST 2 blocks, one HST 2A and one HST 2B. HST 2 blocks are mirrored, so pay close attention to the orientation of each B/C HST prior to placing A3 and sewing.

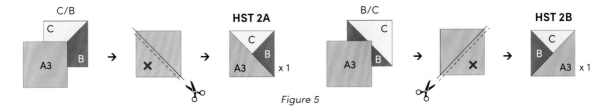

Figure 5

Quilt Assembly

1) To make Row 1, piece together C4 + A/C + C5, as shown in Figure 6.

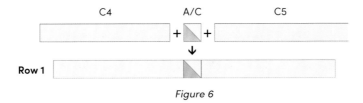

Figure 6

2) To make Row 2, piece together C6 + A/C + C7, as shown in Figure 7.

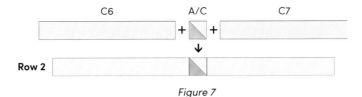

Figure 7

3) To make Row 3, piece together C8 + C/A (right) + A/C + C9 + C/A + C10, as shown in Figure 8.

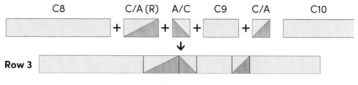

Figure 8

4) To make Row 4, piece together C8 + C/A (right) + A/C + C11 + A/C + C12, as shown in Figure 9.

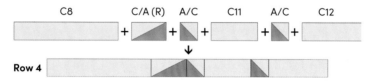

Figure 9

5) To make Row 5, piece together C13 + C/A + A/C (left) + C14 + C/A + A/C + C15, as shown in Figure 10.

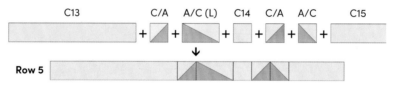

Figure 10

6) To make Row 6, piece together C16 + C/A + C17 + C/A (right) + A/C (left) + C14 + C/A + A/C (left) + C9, as shown in Figure 11.

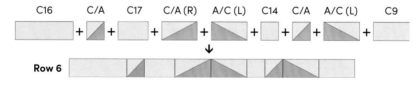

Figure 11

7) To make Row 7, piece together C15 + C/A + A/C (left) + C14 + C/A + A/C (left) + C14 + C/A + A/C + C15, as shown in Figure 12.

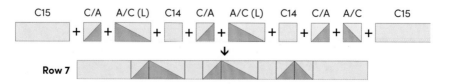

Figure 12

8) To make Row 8, piece together C18 + C/A + A/C (left) + C19 + C/A + A/C + C17 + C/A (right) + A/C + C20, as shown in Figure 13.

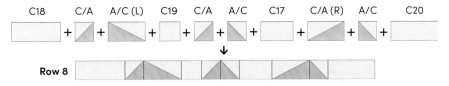

Figure 13

9) To make Row 9, piece together C15 + C/A + A/C + C/B + HRT 3 (right) + HRT 3 (left) + B/C + C/A + A/C (left) + C9, as shown in Figure 14.

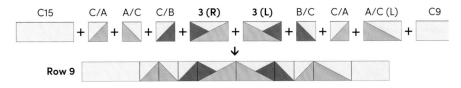

Figure 14

10) To make Row 10, piece together C9 + C/A (right) + HST 2A + B4 + B/A + A/B (left) + B5 + HST 2B + A/C (left) + C9, as shown in Figure 15.

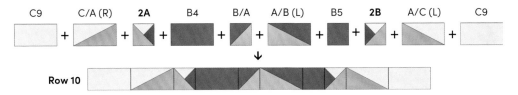

Figure 15

11) To make Row 11, piece together C9 + C/B + B6 + B/A + A/B + B7 + B/A (right) + A/B (left) + B7 + B/A + A/B + B6 + B/C + C9, as shown in Figure 16.

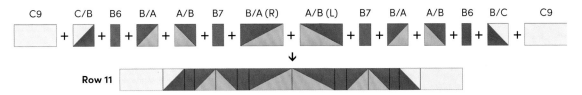

Figure 16

12) To make Row 12, piece together C/B (right) + B5 + B/A + A/B + B8 + B/A + B9 + B/A (right) + A/B + B5 + B/C (left), as shown in Figure 17.

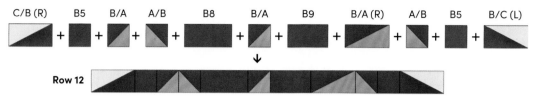

Figure 17

13) To make Block 1, first piece together B10 + A4 + B11, then piece A/B to the top, as shown in Figure 18. To make Block 2, first piece together A4 + B12, then piece A/B to the top, as shown in Figure 19. To make Block 3, first piece together B13 + A4 + B14, then piece B/A to the top, as shown in Figure 20.

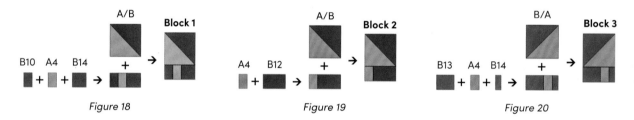

Figure 18   *Figure 19*   *Figure 20*

14) To make Row 13, piece together B15 + Block 1 + B16 + Block 2 + B17 + Block 3 + B18, as shown in Figure 21.

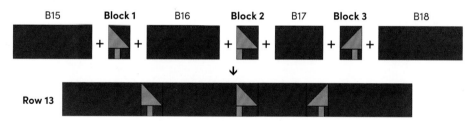

Figure 21

15) Piece together C21 + Rows 1–13, as shown in Figure 22.

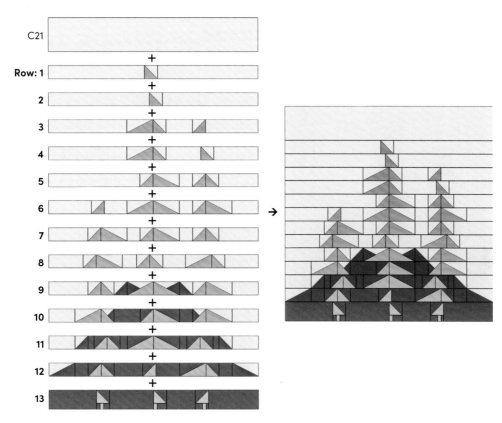

Figure 22

To back and quilt your Rocky Mountain baby quilt, see Assembling Your Quilt (p. 23).

Rocky Mountain Quilt Pattern

Everglades
FLORIDA

Known to Native Americans as Pahayokee, meaning "grass waters," Everglades National Park is located in southern Florida on 1.5 million acres of subtropical wetlands, one of the largest in the world and the only subtropical wilderness area in North America. You can canoe, kayak, and camp along the 99-mile Wilderness Waterway—but keep an eye out for both alligators and crocodiles, as this is one of the few places in the world where they coexist. The Everglades is also home to the Florida panther, once almost extinct; it is one of the few remaining locations in the eastern United States where visitors can see this elusive big cat. This baby quilt recreates the river of grass using curves in green and blue to capture the intricate interconnected channels of wetlands, lakes, and rivers that make up this park.

Finished Measurements | Height: 40 in. (101.6 cm) Width: 40 in. (101.6 cm)

FABRIC: Art Gallery Fabrics *Pure Solids*, 100% cotton
(width: 44 in. [111.75 cm], weight per yard: 4.7 oz)

■ **A** (Night Sea) – 1.375 yards

■ **B** (Dark Citron) – 1.375 yards

BACKING: Any desired
fabric – 2.75 yards

BINDING: Any desired
fabric – .5 yard

NOTIONS: Batting – 48 in.
x 48 in. (122 cm x 122 cm)

TEMPLATES: Everglades A,
Everglades B

Cutting Instructions | BABY QUILT

Note: For more information on cutting and assembling blocks, see p. 14.

■ **A** (Night Sea)

*Cut eight 6 in. (15.2 cm)
x WOF strips. Subcut:*

32 - Template B
8 - 2.5 in. x 5.25 in.
(6.3 cm x 13.3 cm) [A1]
32 - Template A

■ **B** (Dark Citron)

*Cut eight 6 in. (15.2 cm)
x WOF strips. Subcut:*

32 - Template B
1 - 2.5 in. x 12 in.
(6.3 cm x 30.5 cm) [B2]
6 - 2.5 in. x 5.25 in.
(6.3 cm x 13.3 cm) [B1]
32 - Template A

BINDING *Cut five 2.5 in.
(6.3 cm) x WOF strips of the
binding fabric.*

Block Assembly

1) The Everglades National Park quilt uses quarter-curve templates
(A and B). See Quarter-Curves (p. 15) for quarter-curve piecing and
trimming instructions. Refer to Figure 1 to determine the required amount
and fabric combinations of the Template Blocks. Trim Template Blocks to
5.25 in. x 5.25 in. (13.3 cm x 13.3 cm).

A/B
B
A   x 32

B/A
A
B   x 32

Figure 1

Quilt Assembly

1) To make Block 1, piece together B1 + A1 + B1 + A1, as shown in Figure 2. Make two blocks. To make Block 2, piece together A1 + B1 + A1 + B2 + A1 + B1 + A1, as shown in Figure 3.

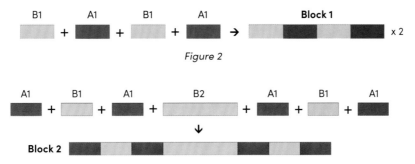

Figure 2

Figure 3

2) To make Block 3, first piece together Template Blocks in the order shown in Figure 4, then piece these rows together.

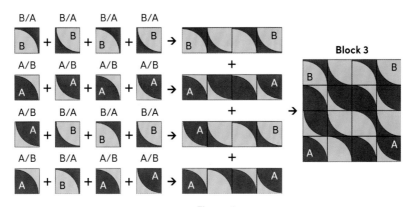

Figure 4

3) To make Block 4, first piece together Template Blocks in the order shown in Figure 5, then piece these rows together.

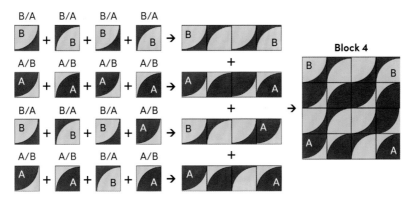

Figure 5

4) To make Block 5, first piece together Template Blocks in the order shown in Figure 6, then piece these rows together.

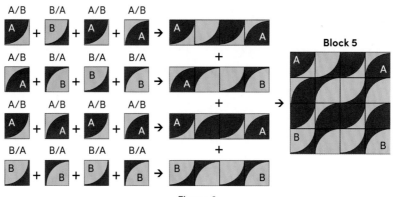

Figure 6

5) To make Block 6, first piece together Template Blocks in the order shown in Figure 7, then piece these rows together.

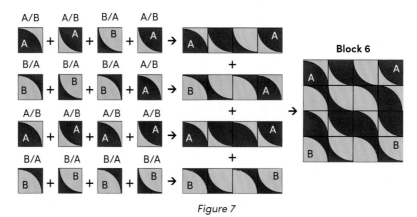

Figure 7

6) To make Block 7, piece together Block 3 + Block 1 + Block 4, as shown in Figure 8. To make Block 8, piece together Block 5 + Block 1 + Block 6, as shown in Figure 9.

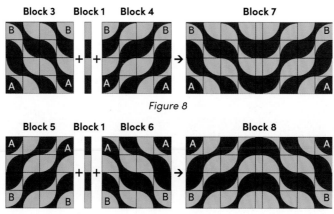

Figure 8

Figure 9

7) Piece together Block 7 + Block 2 + Block 8, as shown in Figure 10.

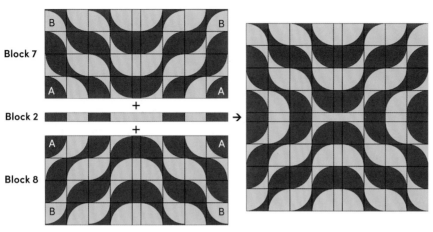

Figure 10

To back and quilt your Everglades baby quilt, see Assembling Your Quilt (p. 23).

Everglades Quilt Pattern

Zion

UTAH

Located in southwestern Utah on 148,000 acres of red rock landscape, Zion National Park has a 2,000-foot-deep canyon that was carved over millions of years and continues to be carved today by the Virgin River. Older rocks were deposited approximately 110 to 270 million years ago and have been weathered and eroded to create a vivid display of ruby, crimson, orange, pink, and cream sedimentary rock layers. You can drive through the Zion–Mt. Carmel Tunnel, which passes through a mile of Zion's sandstone cliffs. One of the park's most popular hikes, considered to be one of the most dangerous in the world, is the 5.4-mile-roundtrip hike of Angels Landing, with sheer drops and exposed edges that provide panoramic views of the Zion Canyon. This baby quilt uses curves, half-rectangle triangles, and half-square triangles in rich sandstone colors to recreate the iconic Angels Landing.

Finished Measurements | Height: 48 in. (121.9 cm) Width: 40 in. (101.6 cm)

FABRIC: Art Gallery Fabrics *Pure Solids*, 100% cotton
(width: 44 in. [111.75 cm], weight per yard: 4.7 oz)

A (Banana Cream) – .33 yard

B (Summer Sun) – .33 yard

C (Autumnal) – .375 yard

D (Undeniably Red) – .5 yard

E (Candied Cherry) – .375 yard

F (Fresh Water) – .67 yard

BACKING: Any desired fabric – 2.75 yards

BINDING: Any desired fabric – .375 yard

NOTIONS: Batting – 48 in. x 56 in. (122 cm x 142.2 cm)

TEMPLATES: Zion A, Zion B

Cutting Instructions | BABY QUILT

Note: For more information on cutting and assembling blocks, see p. 14.

A (Banana Cream)

Cut one 10 in. (25.4 cm) x WOF strip. Subcut:

1 - 10 in. x 10 in. (25.4 cm x 25.4 cm) [A1]

1 - 9.5 in. x 22 in. (24 cm x 55.9 cm) [A2]

B (Summer Sun)

Cut one 9.5 in. (24 cm) x WOF strip. Subcut:

1 - 9.5 in. x 31 in. (24 cm x 78.7 cm) [B1]

C (Autumnal)

Cut one 11.5 in. (29.2 cm) x WOF strip. Subcut:

1 - 5 in. x 11.5 in. (12.7 cm x 29.2 cm) [C1]

1 - 9.5 in. x 31 in. (24 cm x 78.7 cm) [C2]

D (Undeniably Red)

Cut one 9.5 in. (24 cm) x WOF strip. Subcut:

1 - 9.5 in. x 33.5 in. (24 cm x 85.1 cm) [D1]

Cut one 5 in. (12.7 cm) x WOF strip. Subcut:

2 - Template A

E (Candied Cherry)

Cut one 11.5 in. (29.2 cm) x WOF strip. Subcut:

1 - 5 in. x 11.5 in. (12.7 cm x 29.2 cm) [E1]

1 - 9.5 in. x 33.5 in. (24 cm x 85.1 cm) [E2]

F (Fresh Water)

Cut one 10 in. (25.4 cm) x WOF strip. Subcut:

1 - 10 in. x 10 in. (25.4 cm x 25.4 cm) [F2]

1 - 10 in. x 12.5 in. (25.4 cm x 31.7 cm) [F4]

2 - Template B

1 - 2.5 in. x 9.5 in. (6.3 cm x 24 cm) [F5]

1 - 5 in. x 9.5 in. (12.7 cm x 24 cm) [F7]

Cut one 7.5 in. (19 cm) x WOF strip. Subcut:

2 - 7.5 in. x 9.5 in. (19 cm x 24 cm) [F6]

1 - 5 in. x 11.5 in. (12.7 cm x 29.2 cm) [F1]

Cut one 3.5 in. (8.9 cm) x WOF strip. Subcut:

1 - 3.5 in. x 31 in. (8.9 cm x 78.7 cm) [F3]

BINDING *Cut five 2.5 in. (6.3 cm) x WOF strips of the binding fabric.*

Block Assembly

1) The project uses half-curve templates (A and B).
See Half-Curves on p. 14 for half-curve piecing and trimming instructions.
Refer to Figure 1 to determine the required amount of Template Blocks.
Trim Template Blocks to 5 in. x 9.5 in. (12.7 cm x 24 cm).

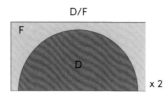

Figure 1

2) For this baby quilt, HRTs are sewn in one orientation (right).
Cut each C1, E1, and F1 rectangle in half diagonally, paying close attention
to the direction each is cut, as shown in Figure 2. Pair each cut triangle
with its corresponding cut triangle, as shown in Figure 3. Refer to Figure 3
to determine the required amount and fabric combinations of HRTs.
See Half-Rectangle Triangles (p. 16) for HRT piecing and trimming instructions.
Trim HRTs to 3 in. x 9.5 in. (7.6 cm x 24 cm).

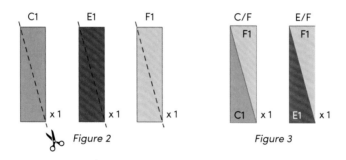

Figure 2   Figure 3

3) To make the HSTs, pair A1 and F2, as shown in Figure 4.
Refer to Figure 4 to determine the required amount of HSTs. See Half-Square
Triangles (p. 19) for two-at-a-time HST piecing and trimming instructions.
Trim HSTs to 9.5 in. x 9.5 in. (24 cm x 24 cm).

Figure 4

Quilt Assembly

1) To make Row 1, first piece together A2 + A/F,
then piece F3 on top and F4 on the right, as shown in Figure 5.

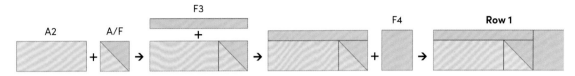

Figure 5

2) To make Row 2, first trim one Template Block to 3.5 in. x 9.5 in. (8.9 cm x 24 cm), as shown
in Figure 6. Next, piece together B1 + D/F (trimmed block) + D/F + F5, as shown in Figure 7.

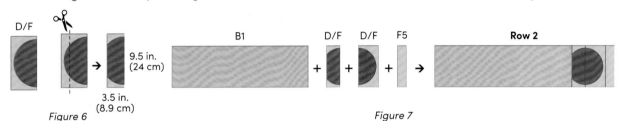

Figure 6   *Figure 7*

3) To make Row 3, piece together C2 + C/F + F6, as shown in Figure 8.

Figure 8

4) To make Row 4, piece together D1 + F6, as shown in Figure 9.

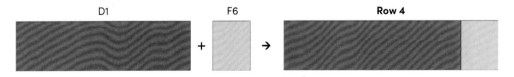

Figure 9

5) To make Row 5, piece together E2 + E/F + F7, as shown in Figure 10.

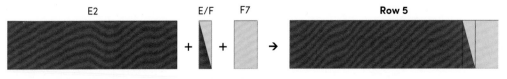

Figure 10

6) Piece together Rows 1–5, as shown in Figure 11.

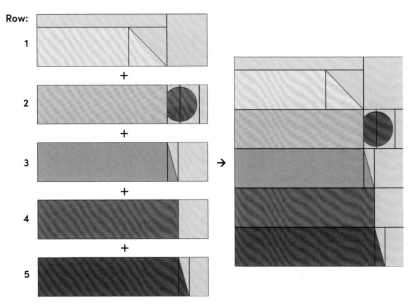

Figure 11

To back and quilt your Zion baby quilt, see Assembling Your Quilt (p. 23).

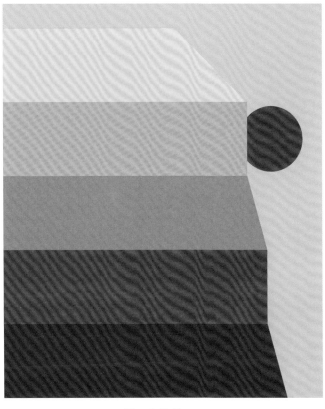

Zion Quilt Pattern

Grand Canyon

ARIZONA

Grand Canyon National Park in Arizona covers 1.2 million acres and is larger than the entire state of Rhode Island. Carved by the Colorado River and its tributaries, the canyon displays some layers of rock that date back 1.8 billion years. The canyon is more than a mile deep and as wide as 18 miles from rim to rim in some locations. You can enjoy taking a scenic drive, hiking, biking, rafting, and kayaking, and you can even take a mule ride into the canyon. This throw quilt captures the ancient rocky layers of the canyon walls, depicted using hues of purple, red, and orange quarter-curves with half-square triangles to represent the Colorado River as it winds its way through the canyon and fades into the glowing sunset.

Finished Measurements | Height: 72 in. (182.9 cm) Width: 72 in. (182.9 cm)

FABRIC: Art Gallery Fabrics *Pure Solids*, 100% cotton
(width: 44 in. [111.75 cm], weight per yard: 4.7 oz)

A (Tranquil Waters) – 1 yard

B (Plum Preserve) – .875 yard

C (Weathered Brick) – .5 yard

D (Chocolate) – .5 yard

E (Sienna Brick) – .67 yard

F (Miami Sunset) – .67 yard

G (Summer Sun) – .67 yard

H (Georgia Peach) – 1.25 yards

I (Aurora Red) – .25 yard

BACKING: Any desired fabric – 4.5 yards

BINDING: Any desired fabric – .625 yard

NOTIONS: Batting – 80 in. x 80 in. (203.2 cm x 203.2 cm)

TEMPLATES: New River Gorge/Grand Canyon 1A, New River Gorge/Grand Canyon 1B,

Acadia 3A/Grand Canyon 2A, Acadia 3B/Grand Canyon 2B

Cutting Instructions | THROW

Note: For more information on cutting and assembling blocks, see p. 14.

A (Tranquil Waters)

Cut five 4.5 in. (11.4 cm) x WOF strips. Subcut:

one strip:

1 - 4.5 in. x 28.5 in. (11.4 cm x 72.4 cm) [A8]

2 - 4.5 in. x 4.5 in. (11.4 cm x 11.4 cm) [A2]

one strip:

1 - 4.5 in. x 24.5 in. (11.4 cm x 62.2 cm) [A7]

1 - 4.5 in. x 16.5 in. (11.4 cm x 42 cm) [A5]

one strip:

1 - 4.5 in. x 24.5 in. (11.4 cm x 62.2 cm) [A7 – 2 total]

1 - 4.5 in. x 16.5 in. (11.4 cm x 42 cm) [A5 – 2 total]

one strip:

2 - 4.5 in. x 20.5 in. (11.4 cm x 52.1 cm) [A6]

one strip:

2 - 4.5 in. x 8.5 in. (11.4 cm x 21.6 cm) [A3]

2 - 4.5 in. x 12.5 in. (11.4 cm x 31.75 cm) [A4]

Cut one 5 in. (12.7 cm) x WOF strip. Subcut:

7 - 5 in. x 5 in. (12.7 cm x 12.7 cm) [A1]

B (Plum Preserve)

Cut two 10.5 in. (26.7 cm) x WOF strips. Subcut:

one strip:

1 - 10.5 in. x 29.5 in. (26.7 cm x 75 cm) [B4]

2 - 5 in. x 5 in. (12.7 cm x 12.7 cm) [B1]

one strip:

1 - 10.5 in. x 29.5 in. (26.7 cm x 75 cm) [B4 – 2 total]

2 - 4.5 in. x 6.5 in. (11.4 cm x 16.5 cm) [B2]

2 - Template 1A

Cut two 4.5 in. (11.4 cm) x WOF strips. Subcut:

2 - 4.5 in. x 21.5 in. (11.4 cm x 54.6 cm) [B3]

C (Weathered Brick)

Cut one 5 in. (12.7 cm) x WOF strip. Subcut:

1 - 5 in. x 5 in. (12.7 cm x 12.7 cm) [C1]

2 - Template 1B

2 - Template 1A

Cut two 4.5 in. (11.4 cm) x WOF strips. Subcut:

one strip:

1 - 4.5 in. x 21.5 in. (11.4 cm x 54.6 cm) [C2]

1 - 4.5 in. x 14.5 in. (11.4 cm x 36.8 cm) [C3]

one strip:

  1 - 4.5 in. x 21.5 in.
  (11.4 cm x 54.6 cm)
  [C2 – 2 total]

  1 - 4.5 in. x 14.5 in.
  (11.4 cm x 36.8 cm)
  [C3 – 2 total]

D (Chocolate)

Cut one 5 in. (12.7 cm)
x WOF strip. Subcut:

  1 - 5 in. x 5 in.
  (12.7 cm x 12.7 cm) [D1]

  2 - Template 1B

  2 - Template 1A

Cut two 4.5 in. (11.4 cm)
x WOF strips. Subcut:

one strip:

  1 - 4.5 in. x 21.5 in.
  (11.4 cm x 54.6 cm) [D2]

  1 - 4.5 in. x 18.5 in.
  (11.4 cm x 47 cm) [D3]

one strip:

  1 - 4.5 in. x 21.5 in.
  (11.4 cm x 54.6 cm)
  [D2 – 2 total]

  1 - 4.5 in. x 18.5 in.
  (11.4 cm x 47 cm)
  [D3 – 2 total]

E (Sienna Brick)

Cut one 5 in. (12.7 cm)
x WOF strip. Subcut:

  1 - 5 in. x 5 in.
  (12.7 cm x 12.7 cm) [E1]

  2 - Template 1B

  2 - Template 1A

Cut four 4.5 in. (11.4 cm)
x WOF strips. Subcut:

  2 - 4.5 in. x 21.5 in.
  (11.4 cm x 54.6 cm) [E2]

  2 - 4.5 in. x 22.5 in.
  (11.4 cm x 57.1 cm) [E3]

F (Miami Sunset)

Cut one 5 in. (12.7 cm)
x WOF strip. Subcut:

  1 - 5 in. x 5 in.
  (12.7 cm x 12.7 cm) [F1]

  2 - Template 1B

  2 - Template 1A

Cut four 4.5 in. (11.4 cm)
x WOF strips. Subcut:

  2 - 4.5 in. x 21.5 in.
  (11.4 cm x 54.6 cm) [F2]

  2 - 4.5 in. x 26.5 in.
  (11.4 cm x 67.3 cm) [F3]

G (Summer Sun)

Cut four 4.5 in. (11.4 cm)
x WOF strips. Subcut:

  2 - 4.5 in. x 21.5 in.
  (11.4 cm x 54.6 cm) [G2]

  2 - 4.5 in. x 30.5 in.
  (11.4 cm x 77.5 cm) [G3]

Cut one 5 in. (12.7 cm)
x WOF strip. Subcut:

  1 - 5 in. x 5 in.
  (12.7 cm x 12.7 cm) [G1]

  2 - Template 1B

  2 - Template 1A

H (Georgia Peach)

Cut one 10 in. (25.4 cm)
x WOF strip. Subcut:

  2 - Template 2B

  2 - Template 1B

Cut one 28.5 in. (72.4 cm)
x WOF strip. Subcut:

  2 - 19.5 in. x 28.5 in.
  (49.5 cm x 72.4 cm) [H3]

Cut one 4.5 in. (11.4 cm)
x WOF strip. Subcut:

  1 - 4.5 in. x 25.5 in.
  (11.4 cm x 64.8 cm) [H1]

  1 - 3.5 in. x 16.5 in.
  (8.9 cm x 42 cm) [H2]

I (Aurora Red)

Cut one 7.5 in. (19 cm)
x WOF strip. Subcut:

  2 - Template 2A

BINDING *Cut eight 2.5 in.*
(6.3 cm) x WOF strips of the
binding fabric.

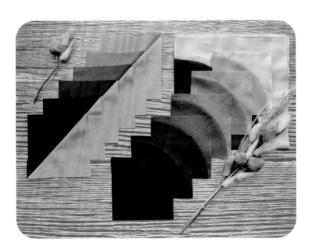

Block Assembly

1) The Grand Canyon National Park quilt uses quarter- and half-curve templates (1A, 1B, 2A, and 2B). See Half-Curves (p. 14) and Quarter-Curves (p. 15) for half- and quarter-curve piecing and trimming instructions. Refer to Figure 1 to determine the required amount and fabric combinations of the Template Blocks. Trim Template Block 1 to 4.5 in. x 4.5 in. (11.4 cm x 11.4 cm) and Template Block 2 to 8.5 in. x 16.5 in. (21.6 cm x 42 cm).

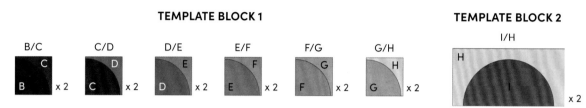

Figure 1

2) To make the HSTs, pair each A1, B1, C1, D1, E1, F1, and G1 square with its corresponding square, as shown in Figure 2. Refer to Figure 2 to determine the required amount and fabric combinations of HSTs. See Half-Square Triangles (p. 19) for two-at-a-time HST piecing and trimming instructions. Trim HSTs to 4.5 in. x 4.5 in. (11.4 cm x 11.4 cm).

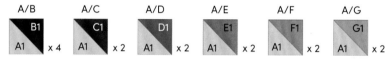

Figure 2

Quilt Assembly

1) To make Block 1A, piece together B2 + B/A.
To make Block 1B, piece together A/B + B2, as shown in Figure 3.

Figure 3

2) To make Block 2A and Block 2B, piece together A2 + A/B + B3 + B/C, as shown in Figure 4.

Figure 4

3) To make Block 3A and Block 3B, piece together A3 + A/C + C2 + C/D, as shown in Figure 5.

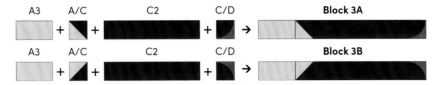

Figure 5

4) To make Block 4A and Block 4B, piece together A4 + A/D + D2 + D/E, as shown in Figure 6.

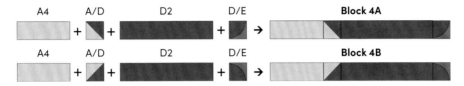

Figure 6

5) To make Block 5A and Block 5B, piece together A5 + A/E + E2 + E/F, as shown in Figure 7.

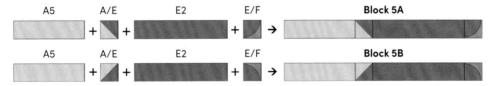

Figure 7

6) To make Block 6A and Block 6B, piece together A6 + A/F + F2 + F/G, as shown in Figure 8.

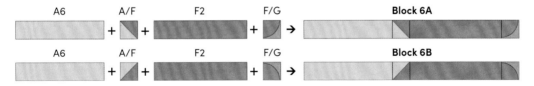

Figure 8

7) To make Block 7A and Block 7B, piece together A7 + A/G + G2 + G/H, as shown in Figure 9.

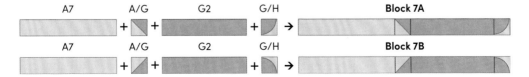

Figure 9

8) To make Block 8, piece together A8 + H1, as shown in Figure 10.

Figure 10

9) To make the Left Block, first piece together B4 + Block 1A, then piece Block 2A to the right of this block. Next, piece C3 to the top, and Block 3A to the right. Continue building the Left Block, sewn log cabin style, alternating D3, E3, F3, and G3 on the top with Blocks 4A, 5A, 6A, and 7A on the right, as shown in Figures 11–13.

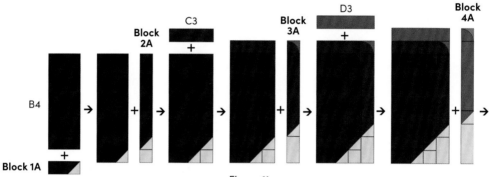

Figure 11

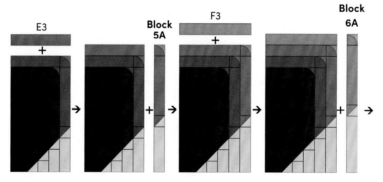

Figure 12

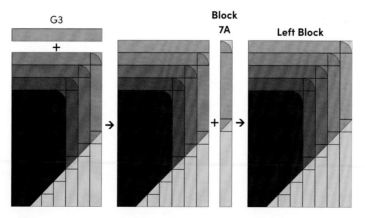

Figure 13

10) To make the Right Block, first piece together B4 + Block 1B, then piece Block 2B to the left of this block. Next, piece C3 to top, then Block 3B to the left. Continue building the Right Block, sewn log cabin style, alternating D3, E3, F3, and G3 on top with Blocks 4B, 5B, 6B, and 7B on the left, as shown in Figures 14–16.

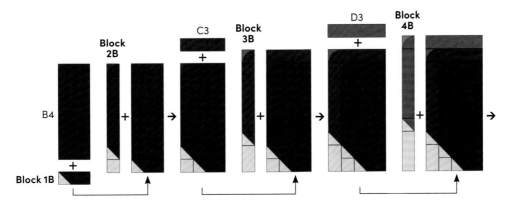

Figure 14

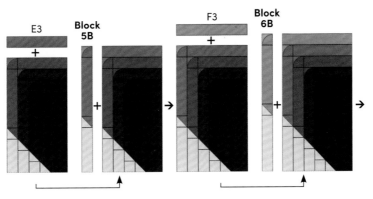

Figure 15

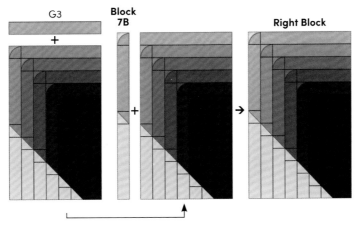

Figure 16

11) To make Block 9, first piece together I/H + I/H, then piece H2 on top, as shown in Figure 17. Next, piece H3 to each side of this block, as shown in Figure 18.

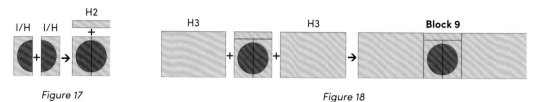

Figure 17

Figure 18

12) Piece together Left Block + Block 8 + Right Block, as shown in Figure 19. Next, piece Block 9 to the top, as shown in Figure 20.

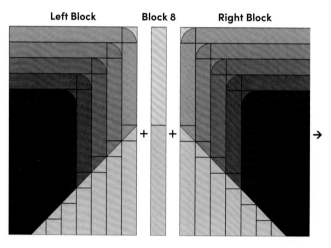

Figure 19

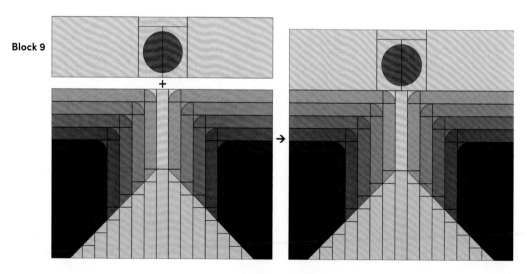

Figure 20

To back and quilt your Grand Canyon throw, see Assembling Your Quilt (p. 23).

Grand Canyon Quilt Pattern

Acadia

MAINE

Maine's Acadia National Park spans 49,000 acres, including 60 miles of Atlantic coastline and 150 miles of hiking trails featuring rocky cliffs, sandy beaches, islands, mountains, and forests harboring more than 1,000 plant species. For a unique experience, walk across the Bar Island Land Bridge at low tide to one of the park's islands, or check out Thunder Hole, a small inlet where the waves crashing into the rocks create a thunderous sound at high tide. Be sure to bring your raincoat, as water can spray as high as 40 feet in the air. This throw quilt captures the scenery of the rugged cliffs at Bass Harbor Head Lighthouse using half-rectangle triangles and half-square triangles as ocean waves crash into curved rocks at sunset.

Finished Measurements | Height: 72 in. (182.9 cm) Width: 60 in. (152.4 cm)

FABRIC: Art Gallery Fabrics *Pure Solids*, 100% cotton
(width: 44 in. [111.75 cm], weight per yard: 4.7 oz)

A (Lava Rock) – 1.125 yards

B (Nocturnal) – .25 yard

C (Heart of the Ocean) – .25 yard

D (Tile Blue) – .25 yard

E (Maldives) – .33 yard

F (Cozumel Blue) – .33 yard

G (Fresh Water) – .33 yard

H (Icy Mint) – .33 yard

I (White Linen) – .33 yard

J (Honeydew) – 1.625 yards

K (Apple Cider) – .25 yard

BACKING: Any desired fabric – 4 yards

BINDING: Any desired fabric – .5 yard

NOTIONS: Batting – 68 in. x 80 in. (172.7 cm x 203.2 cm)

TEMPLATES: Acadia 1A, Acadia 1B, Acadia 2A, Acadia 2B, Acadia 3A/ Grand Canyon 2A, Acadia 3B/Grand Canyon 2B

Cutting Instructions | THROW

Note: For more information on cutting and assembling blocks, see p. 14.

A (Lava Rock)

Cut one 11 in. (28 cm) x WOF strip. Subcut:

2 - 5.5 in. x 11 in. (14 cm x 28 cm) [A1]

1 - 9.5 in. x 11.5 in. (24 cm x 29.2 cm) [A6]

1 - 9.5 in. x 16 in. (24 cm x 40.6 cm) [A7]

Cut one 5.5 in. (14 cm) x WOF strip. Subcut:

3 - 5.5 in. x 5.5 in. (14 cm x 14 cm) [A3]

1 - 5 in. x 24.5 in. (12.7 cm x 62.2 cm) [A10]

Cut three 5 in. (12.7 cm) x WOF strips. Subcut:

one strip:

1 - 5 in. x 20 in. (12.7 cm x 50.8 cm) [A11]

1 - 4.5 in. x 20.5 in. (11.4 cm x 52.1 cm) [A8]

one strip:

1 - 5 in. x 11 in. (12.7 cm x 28 cm) [A12]

1 - 4.5 in. x 22.5 in. (11.4 cm x 57.1 cm) [A9]

1 - 2.5 in. x 3 in. (6.3 cm x 7.6 cm) [A4]

1 - 2.5 in. x 2.5 in. (6.3 cm x 6.3 cm) [A14]

one strip:

1 - 5 in. x 7 in. (12.7 cm x 17.8 cm) [A5]

1 - 5 in. x 6.5 in. (12.7 cm x 16.5 cm) [A13]

3 - Template 2A

1 - Template 1A

Cut one 3.5 in. (8.9 cm) x WOF strip. Subcut:

3 - 3 in. x 6 in. (7.6 cm x 15.2 cm) [A2]

4 - Template 1A (5 total)

B (Nocturnal)

Cut one 6 in. (15.2 cm) x WOF strip. Subcut:

1 - 3 in. x 6 in. (7.6 cm x 15.2 cm) [B1]

1 - 4.5 in. x 38.5 in. (11.4 cm x 97.8 cm) [B2]

C (Heart of the Ocean)

Cut one 6 in. (15.2 cm) x WOF strip. Subcut:

1 - 3 in. x 6 in. (7.6 cm x 15.2 cm) [C1]

1 - 4.5 in. x 36.5 in. (11.4 cm x 92.7 cm) [C2]

D (Tile Blue)

Cut one 5.5 in. (14 cm) x WOF strip. Subcut:

1 - 5.5 in. x 5.5 in. (14 cm x 14 cm) [D1]

1 - 5 in. x 32 in. (12.7 cm x 81.3 cm) [D2]

■ E (Maldives)

Cut one 5.5 in. (14 cm)
x WOF strip. Subcut:

1 - 5.5 in. x 11 in.
(14 cm x 28 cm) [E1]
1 - 1 in. x 10.5 in.
(2.5 cm x 26.7 cm) [E2]
1 - 1 in. x 5 in.
(2.5 cm x 12.7 cm) [E4]

Cut one 5 in. (12.7 cm)
x WOF strip. Subcut:

1 - 5 in. x 21.5 in.
(12.7 cm x 54.6 cm) [E3]
1 - Template 2B

■ F (Cozumel Blue)

Cut one 5.5 in. (14 cm)
x WOF strip. Subcut:

1 - 5.5 in. x 11 in.
(14 cm x 28 cm) [F1]
1 - 5 in. x 30.5 in.
(12.7 cm x 77.5 cm) [F4]

Cut one 5 in. (12.7 cm)
x WOF strip. Subcut:

1 - 5 in. x 5 in.
(12.7 cm x 12.7 cm) [F5]
1 - Template 1B
1 - 1.5 in. x 6.5 in.
(3.8 cm x 16.5 cm) [F2]
1 - 1 in. x 6.5 in.
(2.5 cm x 16.5 cm) [F3]

■ G (Fresh Water)

Cut one 5.5 in. (14 cm)
x WOF strip. Subcut:

1 - 5.5 in. x 5.5 in.
(14 cm x 14 cm) [G1]
1 - 5 in. x 13 in.
(12.7 cm x 33 cm) [G4]
1 - 5 in. x 8 in.
(12.7 cm x 20.3 cm) [G6]

1 - 4.5 in. x 5 in.
(11.4 cm x 12.7 cm) [G7]
1 - Template 2B

Cut one 4 in. (10.2 cm)
x WOF strip. Subcut:

2 - Template 1B
1 - 4 in. x 5 in.
(10.2 cm x 12.7 cm) [G5]
2 - 2 in. x 6.5 in.
(5.1 cm x 16.5 cm) [G3]
1 - 1 in. x 10.5 in.
(2.5 cm x 26.7 cm) [G2]

■ H (Icy Mint)

Cut two 5 in. (12.7 cm)
x WOF strips. Subcut:

one strip:

1 - 5 in. x 19.5 in.
(12.7 cm x 49.5 cm) [H7]
1 - 5 in. x 8 in.
(12.7 cm x 20.3 cm) [H8]
1 - Template 2B

one strip:

1 - 5 in. x 6 in.
(12.7 cm x 15.2 cm) [H9]
2 - Template 1B
1 - 3 in. x 6 in.
(7.6 cm x 15.2 cm) [H1]
1 - 2 in. x 6.5 in.
(5.1 cm x 16.5 cm) [H5]
1 - 3 in. x 6.5 in.
(7.6 cm x 16.5 cm) [H6]
1 - 1.5 in. x 6.5 in.
(3.8 cm x 16.5 cm) [H2]
1 - 1 in. x 6.5 in.
(2.5 cm x 16.5 cm) [H3]
1 - 1 in. x 10.5 in.
(2.5 cm x 26.7 cm) [H4]

□ I (White Linen)

Cut two 5 in. (12.7 cm) x WOF strips.
Sew together, then subcut:

1 - 5 in. x 60.5 in.
(12.7 cm x 153.7 cm) [I1]

□ J (Honeydew)

Cut one 19.5 in. (49.5 cm)
x WOF strip. Subcut:

1 - 10 in. x 19.5 in.
(25.4 cm x 49.5 cm) [J8]
1 - 19.5 in. x 19.5 in.
(49.5 cm x 49.5 cm) [J9]
1 - 4 in. x 16 in.
(10.2 cm x 40.6 cm) [J7]
1 - 5.5 in. x 11 in.
(14 cm x 28 cm) [J1]
1 - 5.5 in. x 5.5 in.
(14 cm x 14 cm) [J3]
1 - 2.5 in. x 9.5 in.
(6.3 cm x 24 cm) [J5]
1 - 3 in. x 6 in.
(7.6 cm x 15.2 cm) [J2]

Cut one 9 in. (22.9 cm)
x WOF strip. Subcut:

2 - Template 3B
1 - 5 in. x 5 in.
(12.7 cm x 12.7 cm) [J6]

Cut three 9.5 in. (24 cm)
x WOF strips. Subcut:

1 - 9.5 in. x 40.5 in.
(24 cm x 102.9 cm) [J10]

Sew two strips together,
then subcut:

1 - 9.5 in. x 60.5 in.
(24 cm x 153.7 cm) [J11]
1 - 3.5 in. x 16.5 in.
(8.9 cm x 42 cm) [J4]

■ K (Apple Cider)

Cut one 7.5 in. (19 cm)
x WOF strip. Subcut:

2 - Template 3A

BINDING Cut seven 2.5 in.
(6.3 cm) x WOF strips of the
binding fabric.

Block Assembly

1) The Acadia National Park quilt uses half-curve templates (1A, 1B, 2A, 2B, 3A, and 3B). See Half-Curves (p. 14) for half-curve piecing and trimming instructions. Refer to Figure 1 to determine the required amount and fabric combinations of the Template Blocks. Trim Template Block 1 to 3.5 in. x 6.5 in. (8.9 cm x 16.5 cm), Template Block 2 to 4.5 in. x 10.5 in. (11.4 cm x 26.7 cm), and Template Block 3 to 8.5 in. x 16.5 in. (21.6 cm x 42 cm).

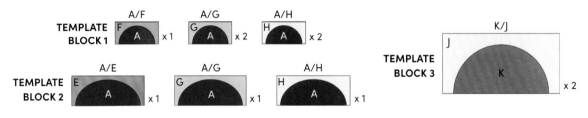

Figure 1

2) HRTs are sewn in two different orientations (right and left). Organize each A1, E1, F1, J1, A2, B1, C1, H1, and J2 rectangle into piles, referring to Figure 2 to determine the required amount for each right/left orientation. Cut each rectangle in half diagonally, paying close attention to the direction each is cut. Keep each HRT in its right/left orientation stack.

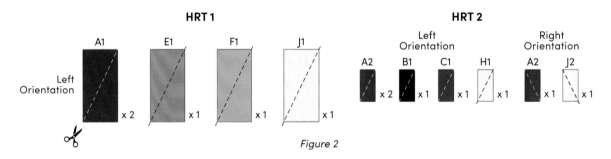

Figure 2

3) Pair each cut triangle with its corresponding cut triangle, as shown in Figure 3. Refer to Figure 3 to determine the required amount and fabric combinations of the HRTs. See Half-Rectangle Triangles (p. 16) for HRT piecing and trimming instructions. Trim HRT 1 to 5 in. x 9.5 in. (12.7 cm x 24 cm) and HRT 2 to 2.5 in. x 4.5 in. (6.3 cm x 11.4 cm).

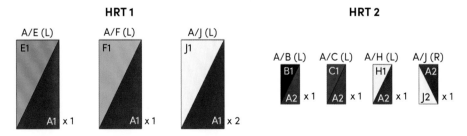

Figure 3

4) To make the HSTs, pair each A3, D1, G1, and J3 square with its corresponding square, as shown in Figure 4. Refer to Figure 4 to determine the required amount and fabric combinations of HSTs. See Half-Square Triangles (p. 19) for two-at-a-time HST piecing and trimming instructions. Trim HSTs to 5 in. x 5 in. (12.7 cm x 12.7 cm).

Figure 4

Quilt Assembly

1) To make Block 1, piece together K/J + K/J + J4, as shown in Figure 5.

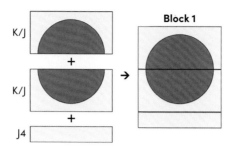

Figure 5

2) To make Block 2, first piece together J5 +J/A (HRT 2 – right) + A4; J6 + J/A + A5; and J/A (HRT 1 – left) + A6. Next, piece these rows together with J7, as shown in Figure 6.

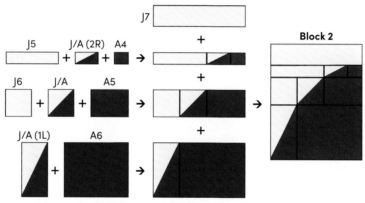

Figure 6

3) To make Row 1, piece together J8 + Block 1 + J9 + Block 2, as shown in Figure 7. To make Row 2, piece together J10 + J/A (HRT 1 – left) + A7, as shown in Figure 8.

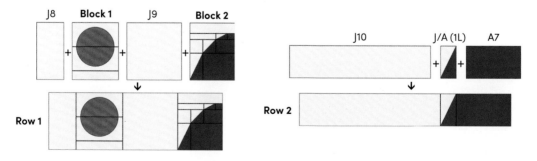

Figure 7   *Figure 8*

4) To make Row 3, piece together B2 + B/A (left) + A8, as shown in Figure 9.
To make Row 4, piece together C2 + C/A (left) + A9, as shown in Figure 10.
To make Row 5, piece together D2 + D/A + A10, as shown in Figure 11.

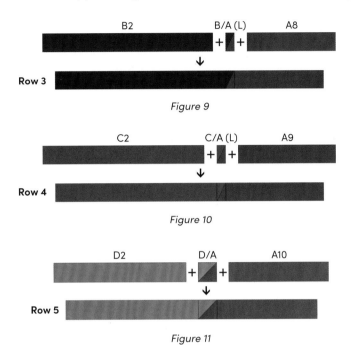

Figure 9

Figure 10

Figure 11

5) To make Block 3, piece together A/E + E2, as shown in Figure 12.
To make Row 6, piece together E3 + Block 3 + E4 + E/A (left) + A11, as shown in Figure 13.

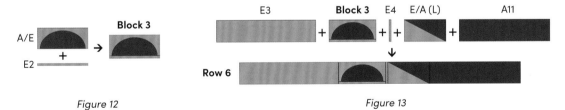

Figure 12

Figure 13

6) To make Block 4, piece together F2 + A/F + F3, as shown in Figure 14.
To make Row 7, piece together F4 + Block 4 + F5 + F/A (left) + A12, as shown in Figure 15.

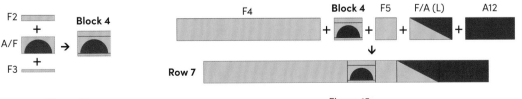

Figure 14

Figure 15

7) To make Block 5, piece together A/G (Template Block 2) + G2, as shown in Figure 16. To make Block 6, piece together G3 + A/G (Template Block 1), as shown in Figure 17. To make Block 7, piece together A/G (Template Block 1) + G3, as shown in Figure 18.

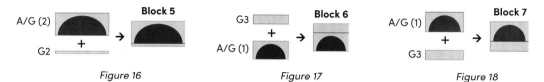

Figure 16   Figure 17   Figure 18

8) To make Row 8, piece together G4 + Block 5 + G5 + Block 6 + G6 + Block 7 + G7 + G/A + A13, as shown in Figure 19.

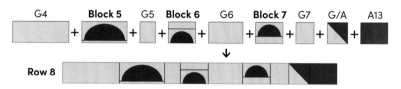

Figure 19

9) To make Block 8, piece together H2 + A/H (Template Block 1) + H3, as shown in Figure 20. To make Block 9, piece together H4 + A/H (Template Block 2), as shown in Figure 21.

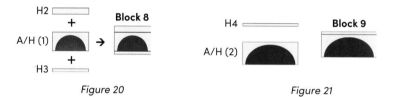

Figure 20   Figure 21

10) To make Block 10, piece together A/H (Template Block 1) + H5, as shown in Figure 22. To make Block 11, first piece together H/A (left) + A14, then piece H6 to the bottom, as shown in Figure 23.

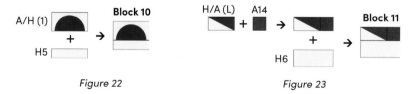

Figure 22   Figure 23

11) To make Row 9, piece together H7 + Block 8 + H8 + Block 9 + H9 + Block 10 + Block 11, as shown in Figure 24.

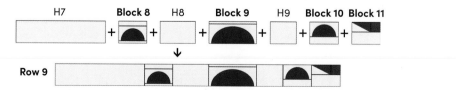

Figure 24

12) Piece together J11 + Rows 1–9 + I1, as shown in Figure 25.

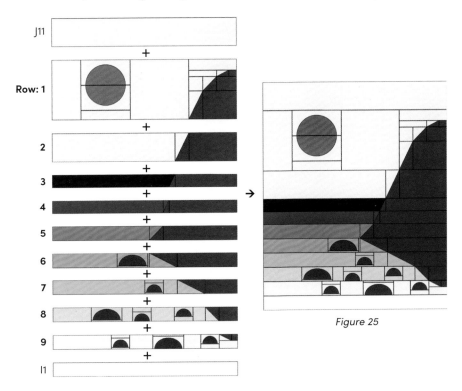

Figure 25

To back and quilt your Acadia throw, see Assembling Your Quilt (p. 23).

Acadia Quilt Pattern

Glacier Bay

ALASKA

At 3.3 million acres in southeast Alaska, Glacier Bay National Park is as large as Yellowstone and Yosemite combined. More than 1,000 glaciers cover 27 percent of the park; the ice that breaks off these glaciers is between 75 and 200 years old. Much of the park is relatively inaccessible but can be reached by small plane or boat, with 90 percent of park visitors arriving by cruise ship. Popular park activities include boat tours, kayaking, fishing, glacier viewing, and whale watching. This throw quilt uses half-rectangle triangles and half-square triangles to recreate the ice-sculpted fjords and snowcapped mountains reflected in the icy blue waters of this rugged terrain.

Finished Measurements | Height: 72 in. (182.9 cm) Width: 60 in. (152.4 cm)

FABRIC: Art Gallery Fabrics *Pure Solids*, 100% cotton
(width: 44 in. [111.75 cm], weight per yard: 4.7 oz)

■ **A** (Evergreen) – 1.25 yards

▨ **B** (Ocean Fog) – 1.33 yards

☐ **C** (White Linen) – 2.5 yards

BACKING: Any desired fabric – 4 yards

BINDING: Any desired fabric – .5 yard

NOTIONS: Batting – 68 in. x 80 in. (172.7 cm x 203.2 cm)

Cutting Instructions | THROW

Note: For more information on cutting and assembling blocks, see p. 14.

■ A (Evergreen)

Cut one 8.5 in. (21.6 cm) x WOF strip. Subcut:

2 – 4.25 in. x 8.5 in. (10.8 cm x 21.6 cm) [A2]
6 – 3.25 in. x 6.5 in. (8.2 cm x 16.5 cm) [A1]
8 – 3.25 in. x 3.25 in. (8.2 cm x 8.2 cm) [A3]

Cut one 6.5 in. (16.5 cm) x WOF strip. Subcut:

12 – 3.25 in. x 6.5 in. (8.2 cm x 16.5 cm) [A1 – 18 total]

Cut one 3.25 in. (8.2 cm) x WOF strip. Subcut:

11 – 3.25 in. x 3.25 in. (8.2 cm x 8.2 cm) [A3 – 19 total]

Cut eight 2.75 in. (7 cm) x WOF strips. Sew three strips together, then subcut:

2 – 2.75 in. x 60.5 in. (7 cm x 153.7 cm) [A9]

one strip:

1 – 2.75 in. x 29 in. (7 cm x 73.7 cm) [A8]
2 – 2.75 in. x 5 in. (7 cm x 12.7 cm) [A5]

one strip:

1 – 2.75 in. x 29 in. (7 cm x 73.7 cm) [A8 – 2 total]
2 – 2.75 in. x 5 in. (7 cm x 12.7 cm) [A5]

one strip:

2 – 2.75 in. x 14 in. (7 cm x 35.5 cm) [A6]
2 – 2.75 in. x 5 in. (7 cm x 12.7 cm) [A5]

one strip:

2 – 2.75 in. x 14 in. (7 cm x 35.5 cm) [A6 – 4 total]
2 – 2.75 in. x 5 in. (7 cm x 12.7 cm) [A5]

one strip:

2 – 2.75 in. x 7.25 in. (7 cm x 18.4 cm) [A7]
2 – 2.75 in. x 5 in. (7 cm x 12.7 cm) [A5 – 10 total]
2 – 2.75 in. x 2.75 in. (7 cm x 7 cm) [A4]

▨ B (Ocean Fog)

Cut one 8.5 in. (21.6 cm) x WOF strip. Subcut:

4 – 4.25 in. x 8.5 in. (10.8 cm x 21.6 cm) [B2]
14 – 3.25 in. x 3.25 in. (8.2 cm x 8.2 cm) [B3]

Cut two 6.5 in. (16.5 cm) x WOF strips. Subcut:

22 – 3.25 in. x 6.5 in. (8.2 cm x 16.5 cm) [B1]

Cut one 3.25 in. (8.2 cm) x WOF strip. Subcut:

8 – 3.25 in. x 3.25 in. (8.2 cm x 8.2 cm) [B3 – 22 total]
2 – 2.75 in. x 7.25 in. (7 cm x 18.4 cm) [B5]

Cut seven 2.75 in. (7 cm) x WOF strips. Sew three strips together, then subcut:

2 – 2.75 in. x 51.5 in. (7 cm x 130.8 cm) [B9]

one strip:

> **7** – 2.75 in. x 5 in.
> (7 cm x 12.7 cm) [B4]
>
> **2** – 2 in. x 2.75 in.
> (5.1 cm x 7 cm) [B7]

one strip:

> **5** – 2.75 in. x 5 in.
> (7 cm x 12.7 cm)
> [B4 – 12 total]
>
> **2** – 2.75 in. x 7.25 in.
> (7 cm x 18.4 cm)
> [B5 – 4 total]

one strip:

> **4** – 2.75 in. x 9.5 in.
> (7 cm x 24 cm) [B8]

one strip:

> **2** – 2.75 in. x 20.75 in.
> (7 cm x 52.7 cm) [B6]

☐ **C** (White Linen)

Cut two 6.5 in. (16.5 cm)
x WOF strips. Subcut:

> **24** – 3.25 in. x 6.5 in.
> (8.2 cm x 16.5 cm) [C1]
>
> **2** – 2 in. x 5 in.
> (5.1 cm x 12.7 cm) [C16]

Cut three 3.25 in. (8.2 cm)
x WOF strips. Subcut:

> **25** – 3.25 in. x 3.25 in.
> (8.2 cm x 8.2 cm) [C3]
>
> **2** – 2.75 in. x 2.75 in.
> (7 cm x 7 cm) [C14]
>
> **2** – 2.75 in. x 16.25 in.
> (7 cm x 41.3 cm) [C5]
>
> **1** – 2 in. x 5 in.
> (5.1 cm x 12.7 cm) [C16]

Cut one 8.5 in. (21.6 cm)
x WOF strip. Subcut:

> **2** – 4.25 in. x 8.5 in.
> (10.8 cm x 21.6 cm) [C2]

> **1** – 8 in. x 11.75 in.
> (20.3 cm x 29.8 cm) [C18]
>
> **7** – 2.75 in. x 8 in.
> (7 cm x 20.3 cm) [C13]
>
> **1** – 2 in. x 5 in.
> (5.1 cm x 12.7 cm) [C16]

Cut one 8 in. (20.3 cm)
x WOF strip. Subcut:

> **1** – 8 in. x 11.75 in.
> (20.3 cm x 29.8 cm)
> [C18 – 2 total]
>
> **2** – 8 in. x 12.5 in.
> (20.3 cm x 31.7 cm) [C17]
>
> **1** – 2.75 in. x 8 in.
> (7 cm x 20.3 cm)
> [C13 – 8 total]
>
> **1** – 2 in. x 5 in.
> (5.1 cm x 12.7 cm) [C16]

Cut thirteen 2.75 in. (7 cm)
x WOF strips. Sew three strips
together, then subcut:

> **2** – 2.75 in. x 60.5 in.
> (7 cm x 153.7 cm) [C10]

one strip:

> **2** – 2.75 in. x 9.5 in.
> (7 cm x 24 cm) [C9]
>
> **2** – 2.75 in. x 11 in.
> (7 cm x 28 cm) [C6]

one strip:

> **1** – 2.75 in. x 11.75 in.
> (7 cm x 29.8 cm) [C7]
>
> **1** – 2.75 in. x 27.5 in.
> (7 cm x 69.8 cm) [C12]

one strip:

> **1** – 2.75 in. x 11.75 in.
> (7 cm x 29.8 cm) [C7]
>
> **1** – 2.75 in. x 27.5 in.
> (7 cm x 69.8 cm) [C12]

one strip:

> **1** – 2.75 in. x 11.75 in.
> (7 cm x 29.8 cm) [C7]

> **1** – 2.75 in. x 27.5 in.
> (7 cm x 69.8 cm) [C12]

one strip:

> **1** – 2.75 in. x 11.75 in.
> (7 cm x 29.8 cm)
> [C7 – 4 total]
>
> **1** – 2.75 in. x 27.5 in.
> (7 cm x 69.8 cm)
> [C12 – 4 total]

one strip:

> **3** – 2.75 in. x 12.5 in.
> (7 cm x 31.7 cm) [C11]
>
> **1** – 2.75 in. x 2.75 in.
> (7 cm x 7 cm) [C14]

one strip:

> **3** – 2.75 in. x 12.5 in.
> (7 cm x 31.7 cm) [C11]
>
> **1** – 2.75 in. x 2.75 in.
> (7 cm x 7 cm) [C14 – 4 total]

one strip:

> **2** – 2.75 in. x 12.5 in.
> (7 cm x 31.7 cm)
> [C11 – 8 total]
>
> **2** – 2.75 in. x 5 in.
> (7 cm x 12.7 cm) [C8]
>
> **1** – 2 in. x 5 in.
> (5.1 cm x 12.7 cm)
> [C16 – 6 total]

two strips:

> **2** – 2.75 in. x 40.25 in.
> (7 cm x 102.2 cm) [C4]

Cut six 2 in. (5.1 cm)
x WOF strips. Sew together,
then subcut:

> **4** – 2 in. x 60.5 in.
> (5.1 cm x 153.7 cm) [C15]

BINDING Cut seven 2.5 in.
(6.3 cm) x WOF strips of the
binding fabric.

Block Assembly

1) To make the HSTs, pair each A3, B3, and C3 square with its corresponding square, as shown in Figure 1. Refer to Figure 1 to determine the required amount and fabric combinations of HSTs. See Half-Square Triangles (p. 19) for two-at-a-time HST piecing and trimming instructions. Trim HSTs to 2.75 in. x 2.75 in. (7 cm x 7 cm).

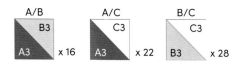

Figure 1

2) After trimming the HSTs, take two B/C HSTs and pair each with an A4 square. Place A4 on top of a B/C HST and draw a diagonal line through the block, perpendicular to the B/C seam, as shown in Figure 2. Sew directly on the marked center line. Trim a .25 in. (.6 cm) seam allowance on the dotted line toward the side of the HST with the red X and press the seams open. Discard the trimmed piece. Make two HST 2 blocks, one HST 2A and one HST 2B. HST 2 blocks are mirrored, so pay close attention to the orientation of each B/C HST prior to placing A4 and sewing.

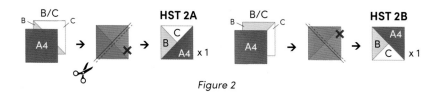

Figure 2

3) HRTs are sewn in two different orientations (right and left). Organize each A1, B1, C1, A2, B2, and C2 rectangle into piles, referring to Figure 3 to determine the required amount for each right/left orientation. Cut each rectangle in half diagonally, paying close attention to the direction each is cut. Keep each HRT in its right/left orientation stack.

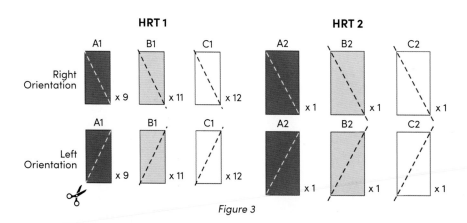

Figure 3

4) Pair each cut triangle with its corresponding cut triangle, as shown in Figure 4. Refer to Figure 4 to determine the required amount and fabric combinations of the HRTs. See Half-Rectangle Triangles (p. 16) for HRT piecing and trimming instructions. Trim HRT 1 to 2.75 in. x 5 in. (7 cm x 12.7 cm) and HRT 2 to 3.25 in. x 6.5 in. (8.2 cm x 16.5 cm).

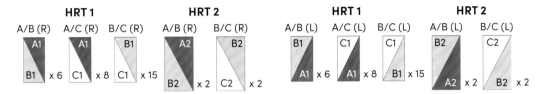

Figure 4

5) To make HRT 3, cut the required amount of trimmed HRT 2 blocks in half on the diagonal noting each orientation, as shown in Figure 5. Discard the triangle with the red X and align each HRT 2 triangle with the remaining A1 and B1 triangles. Make two HRT 3A (left) HRTs, two HRT 3A (right) HRTs, and one left and one right orientation for HRT 3B and HRT 3C. Trim HRT 3 to 2.75 in. x 5 in. (7 cm x 12.7 cm).

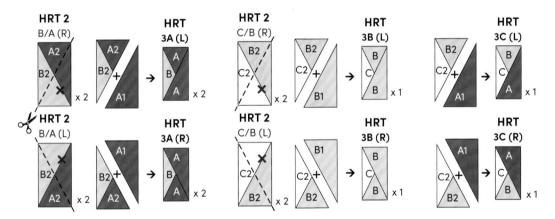

Figure 5

Quilt Assembly

1) To make Rows 1–6, piece blocks together in the order shown in Figure 6.
Rows 3 and 5 will be longer than the other rows.

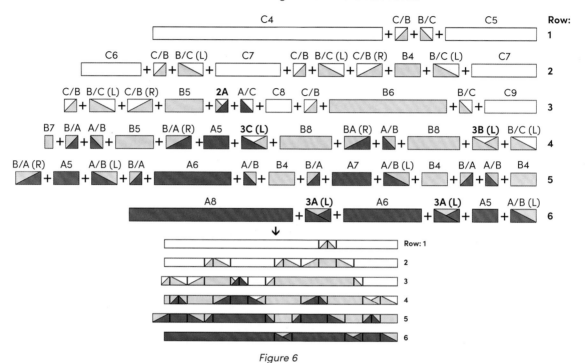

Figure 6

2) To make Rows 7–12, piece blocks together in the order shown in Figure 7.
Rows 8 and 10 will be longer than the other rows.

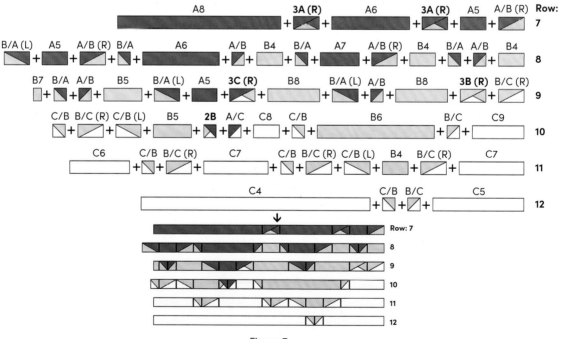

Figure 7

3) To make Block 1, piece together C10 + Rows 1–6 + A9, as shown in Figure 8.
Align the rows and pieces on the right side, with Rows 3 and 5 extending to the left.
To make Block 2, piece together A9 + Rows 7–12 + C10, as shown in Figure 9.
Align the rows and pieces on the right side, with Rows 8 and 10 extending to the left.

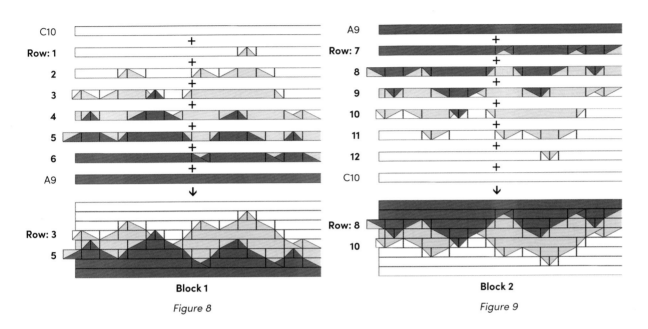

Block 1

Figure 8

Block 2

Figure 9

4) Trim excess fabric from Block 1 (Rows 3 and 5) and Block 2 (Rows 8 and 10), as shown in Figure 10.

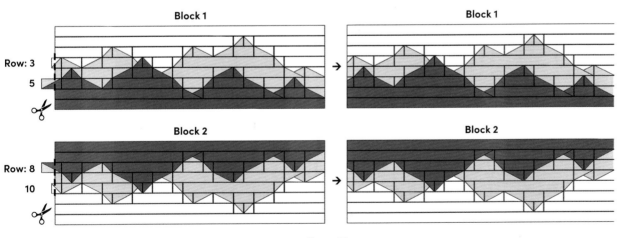

Figure 10

5) To make Rows 13–17, piece blocks together in the order shown in Figure 11. Make two of each row.

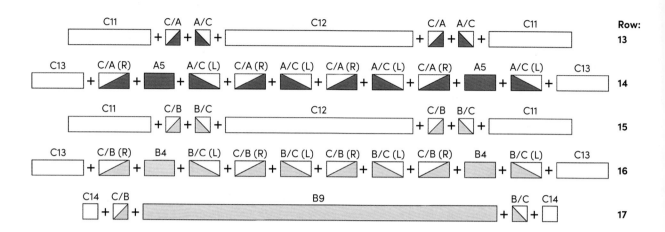

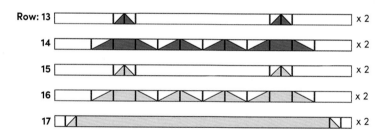

Figure 11

6) To make Block 3, piece together C15 + Rows 13–14 + C15 + Rows 15–17, as shown in Figure 12. Make two blocks.

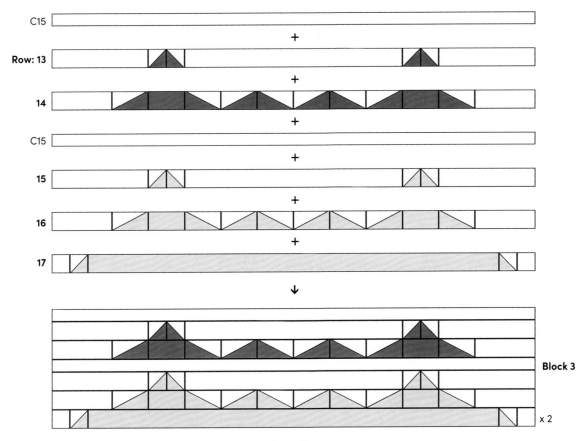

Figure 12

7) To make Block 4, first piece together four A/C HSTs, two on the top and two on the bottom, then piece blocks together, as shown in Figure 13. Next, sew C16 on the top and bottom of this block. Make three blocks.

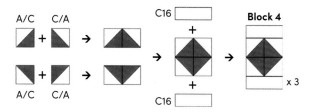

Figure 13

8) To make Block 5, piece together C17 + Block 4 + C18 + Block 4 + C18 + Block 4 + C17, as shown in Figure 14.

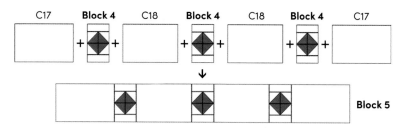

Figure 14

9) Piece together Block 1 + Block 3 + Block 5 + Block 3 + Block 2, as shown in Figure 15.

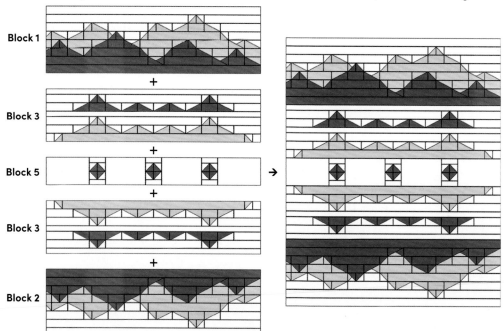

Figure 15

To back and quilt your Glacier Bay throw, see Assembling Your Quilt (p. 23).

Glacier Bay Quilt Pattern

Joshua Tree

CALIFORNIA

Named after the distinct plants found around the park, Joshua Tree National Park sits on 790,000 acres in Southern California and is home to two deserts, the Mojave and the Colorado. Don't let the desert climate fool you, though; it's not unusual to get a dusting of snow during the winter months. In addition to climbing the unique rock formations and hiking and observing the nearly 800 plant species, you can go birdwatching, explore a mine, or just stargaze the night away. While most mountain ranges in the United States run north to south, five of the six ranges in Joshua Tree run east to west. Using curves, half-rectangle triangles, and half-square triangles, this throw quilt captures the spiky, twisted, gnarled branches of a Joshua tree at sunrise with the cool blue tones of a mountain range off in the distance.

Finished Measurements | Height: 72 in. (182.9 cm) Width: 60 in. (152.4 cm)

FABRIC: Art Gallery Fabrics *Pure Solids*, 100% cotton
(width: 44 in. [111.75 cm], weight per yard: 4.7 oz)

A (Cabernet) – .875 yard

B (Aurora Red) – .875 yard

C (Coral Reef) – .875 yard

D (Burnt Orange) – .75 yard

E (Summer Sun) – .5 yard

F (Canary) – .5 yard

G (Honeydew) – .375 yard

H (Tile Blue) – .375 yard

I (Evergreen) – .5 yard

BACKING: Any desired fabric – 4 yards

BINDING: Any desired fabric – .5 yard

NOTIONS: Batting – 68 in. x 80 in. (172.7 cm x 203.2 cm)

TEMPLATES: Joshua Tree 1A, Joshua Tree 1B, Joshua Tree 2A, Joshua Tree 2B

Cutting Instructions | THROW

Note: For more information on cutting and assembling blocks, see p. 14.

A (Cabernet)

Cut one 11 in. (28 cm) x WOF strip. Subcut:

- **5** - 5.5 in. x 11 in. (14 cm x 28 cm) [A1]
- **4** - 5.5 in. x 5.5 in. (14 cm x 14 cm) [A2]

Cut two 5.5 in. (14 cm) x WOF strips. Subcut:

- **5** - 5.5 in. x 5.5 in. (14 cm x 14 cm) [A2 – 9 total]
- **1** - 5 in. x 14 in. (12.7 cm x 35.5 cm) [A5]
- **3** - Template 2A

Cut one 5 in. (12.7 cm) x WOF strip. Subcut:

- **6** - 5 in. x 5 in. (12.7 cm x 12.7 cm) [A3]
- **1** - 5 in. x 9.5 in. (12.7 cm x 24 cm) [A4]

Cut one 2.75 in. (7 cm) x WOF strip. Subcut:

- **6** - Template 1A

B (Aurora Red)

Cut two 14 in. (35.5 cm) x WOF strips. Sew together, then subcut:

- **1** - 14 in. x 60.5 in. (35.5 cm x 153.7 cm) [B1]

C (Coral Reef)

Cut two 14 in. (35.5 cm) x WOF strips. Subcut:

one strip:

- **1** - 14 in. x 17.5 in. (35.5 cm x 44.4 cm) [C5]
- **1** - 5 in. x 5 in. (12.7 cm x 12.7 cm) [C3]
- **1** - 2.5 in. x 5 in. (6.3 cm x 12.7 cm) [C2]
- **1** - 5 in. x 18.5 in. (12.7 cm x 47 cm) [C4]

- **1** - Template 1B
- **1** - Template 2B

one strip:

- **1** - 14 in. x 25.5 in. (35.5 cm x 64.8 cm) [C6]
- **1** - 5.5 in. x 11 in. (14 cm x 28 cm) [C1]

D (Burnt Orange)

Cut one 14 in. (35.5 cm) x WOF strip. Subcut:

- **1** - 10.5 in. x 14 in. (26.7 cm x 35.5 cm) [D8]
- **1** - 14 in. x 14 in. (35.5 cm x 35.5 cm) [D9]
- **2** - 5.5 in. x 11 in. (14 cm x 28 cm) [D1]
- **1** - 5 in. x 12 in. (12.7 cm x 30.5 cm) [D7]

Cut one 5.5 in. (14 cm) x WOF strip. Subcut:

- **5** - 5.5 in. x 5.5 in. (14 cm x 14 cm) [D2]

Cut one 5 in. (12.7 cm)
x WOF strip. Subcut:

1 – 5 in. x 5 in.
(12.7 cm x 12.7 cm) [D3]

1 – 3 in. x 5 in.
(7.6 cm x 12.7 cm) [D4]

1 – 2.5 in. x 5 in.
(6.3 cm x 12.7 cm) [D5]

1 – 5 in. x 7.5 in.
(12.7 cm x 19 cm) [D6]

4 – Template 1B

 **E** (Summer Sun)

Cut one 11 in. (28 cm)
x WOF strip. Subcut:

1 – 5.5 in. x 11 in.
(14 cm x 28 cm) [E1]

2 – 5.5 in. x 5.5 in.
(14 cm x 14 cm) [E2]

1 – 9.5 in. x 21 in.
(24 cm x 53.3 cm) [E5]

2 – Template 2B

Cut one 5 in. (12.7 cm)
x WOF strip. Subcut:

1 – 5 in. x 5 in.
(12.7 cm x 12.7 cm) [E3]

1 – 4 in. x 9.5 in.
(10.2 cm x 24 cm) [E4]

 **F** (Canary)

Cut one 11 in. (28 cm)
x WOF strip. Subcut:

1 – 5.5 in. x 11 in.
(14 cm x 28 cm) [F1]

3 – 5.5 in. x 5.5 in.
(14 cm x 14 cm) [F2]

1 – 2.5 in. x 5 in.
(6.3 cm x 12.7 cm) [F3]

1 – 5 in. x 13 in.
(12.7 cm x 33 cm) [F4]

1 – 5 in. x 22 in.
(12.7 cm x 55.9 cm) [F5]

1 – Template 1B

Cut one 5 in. (12.7 cm)
x WOF strip. Subcut:

2 – 5 in. x 16.5 in.
(12.7 cm x 42 cm) [F6]

 **G** (Honeydew)

Cut one 11 in. (28 cm)
x WOF strip. Subcut:

2 – 5.5 in. x 11 in.
(14 cm x 28 cm) [G1]

1 – 5.5 in. x 5.5 in.
(14 cm x 14 cm) [G2]

1 – 5 in. x 13 in.
(12.7 cm x 33 cm) [G3]

1 – 5 in. x 8.5 in.
(12.7 cm x 21.6 cm) [G4]

1 – 5 in. x 10 in.
(12.7 cm x 25.4 cm) [G5]

1 – 5 in. x 5.5 in.
(12.7 cm x 14 cm) [G6]

 **H** (Tile Blue)

Cut one 11 in. (28 cm)
x WOF strip. Subcut:

4 – 5.5 in. x 11 in.
(14 cm x 28 cm) [H1]

4 – 5.5 in. x 5.5 in.
(14 cm x 14 cm) [H2]

1 – 5 in. x 5 in.
(12.7 cm x 12.7 cm) [H3]

 **I** (Evergreen)

Cut one 11 in. (28 cm)
x WOF strip. Subcut:

2 – 5.5 in. x 11 in.
(14 cm x 28 cm) [I1]

2 – 5.5 in. x 5.5 in.
(14 cm x 14 cm) [I2]

1 – 5 in. x 20.5 in.
(12.7 cm x 52.1 cm) [I5]

Cut one 5 in. (12.7 cm)
x WOF strip. Subcut:

1 – 5 in. x 5 in.
(12.7 cm x 12.7 cm) [I3]

1 – 5 in. x 7 in.
(12.7 cm x 17.8 cm) [I4]

1 – 5 in. x 25 in.
(12.7 cm x 63.5 cm) [I6]

BINDING Cut seven 2.5 in.
(6.3 cm) x WOF strips of the
binding fabric.

Block Assembly

1) The Joshua Tree National Park quilt uses half-curve templates (1A, 1B, 2A, and 2B). See Half-Curves on p. 14 for half-curve piecing and trimming instructions. Refer to Figure 1 to determine the required amount and fabric combinations of the Template Blocks. Trim Template Block 1 to 3 in. x 5 in. (7.6 cm x 12.7 cm) and Template Block 2 to 5 in. x 9.5 in. (12.7 cm x 24 cm).

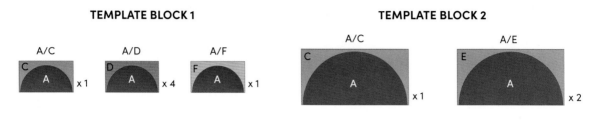

Figure 1

2) HRTs are sewn in two different orientations (right and left). Organize each A1, C1, D1, E1, F1, G1, H1, and I1 rectangle into piles, referring to Figure 2 to determine the required amount for each right/left orientation. Cut each rectangle in half diagonally, paying close attention to the direction each is cut. Keep each HRT in its right/left orientation stack.

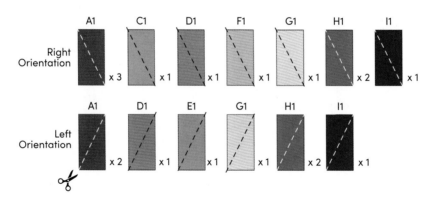

Figure 2

3) Pair each cut triangle with its corresponding cut triangle, as shown in Figure 3. Refer to Figure 3 to determine the required amount and fabric combinations of HRTs. See Half-Rectangle Triangles (p. 16) for HRT piecing and trimming instructions. Trim HRTs to 5 in. x 9.5 in. (12.7 cm x 24 cm).

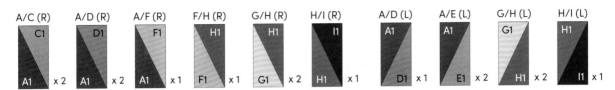

Figure 3

4) To make the HSTs, pair each A2, D2, E2, F2, G2, H2, and I2 square with its corresponding square, as shown in Figure 4. Refer to Figure 4 to determine the required amount and fabric combinations of HSTs. See Half-Square Triangles (p. 19) for two-at-a-time HST piecing and trimming instructions. Trim HSTs to 5 in. x 5 in. (12.7 cm x 12.7 cm).

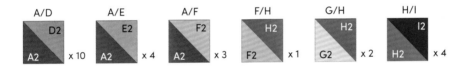

Figure 4

5) After trimming the HSTs, take three A/D HSTs and pair each with an A3 square. Place A3 on top of an A/D HST and draw a diagonal line through the block, perpendicular to the A/D seam, as shown in Figure 5. Sew directly on the marked center line. Trim a .25 in. (.6 cm) seam allowance on the dotted line toward the side of the HST with the red X and press the seams open. Discard the trimmed piece. Make three HST 2 blocks.

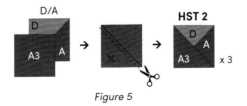

Figure 5

Quilt Assembly

1) **To make Block 1,** first piece together C2 + A/C (Template Block 1), then piece C3 to the bottom, as shown in Figure 6. To make Block 2, piece together A/C (Template Block 2) + A/C (right) + Block 1 + A/C (right), as shown in Figure 7. To make Block 3, piece together C4 + Block 2, as shown in Figure 8.

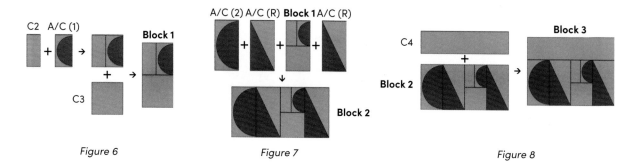

Figure 6

Figure 7

Figure 8

2) **To make Row 1,** piece together C5 + Block 3 + C6, as shown in Figure 9.

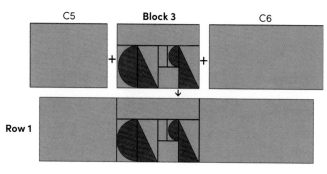

Figure 9

3) **To make Block 4,** first piece together A/D (Template Block 1) + A/D + D3; D4 + D/A (left); and A/D (Template Block 1) + A/D + D/A. Next, piece these rows together, as shown in Figure 10. To make Block 5, piece together D5 + A/D (Template Block 1), as shown in Figure 11.

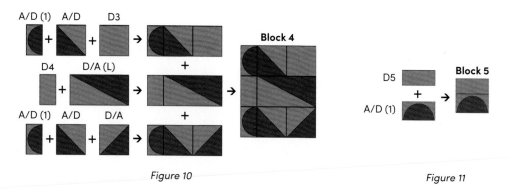

Figure 10

Figure 11

4) To make Block 6, first piece together D/A + HST 2 + A/D; HST 2 + A/D (right); and A/D + Block 5 + D/A. Next, piece these rows together, as shown in Figure 12. To make Block 7, first piece together D/A (right) + A/D (Template Block 1); then HST 2 + D6. Next, piece these rows together with D7 on top, as shown in Figure 13.

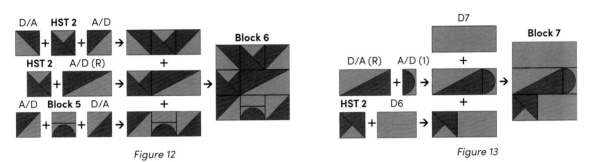

Figure 12

Figure 13

5) To make Row 2, piece together D8 + Block 4 + Block 6 + Block 7 + D9, as shown in Figure 14.

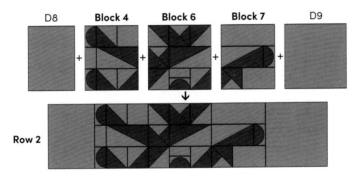

Figure 14

6) To make Block 8, piece together A/E (Template Block 2) + E/A (left), as shown in Figure 15. To make Block 9, first piece together E/A (left) + A/E, and A3 + A/E + A3. Next, piece these rows together, as shown in Figure 16.

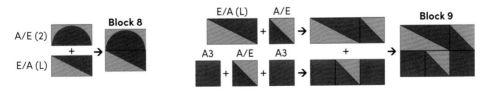

Figure 15

Figure 16

7) To make Block 10, first piece together A3 + A/E + E3, then A/E + A/E (Template Block 2). Next, piece these rows together, as shown in Figure 17. To make Row 3, piece together E4 + Block 8 + Block 9 + Block 10 + E5, as shown in Figure 18.

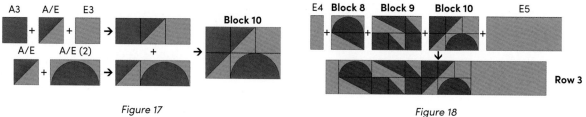

Figure 17

Figure 18

8) To make Block 11, piece together A/F (Template Block 1) + F3, as shown in Figure 19. To make Block 12, first piece together F4 + Block 11 + F/A, then piece F5 to the bottom, as shown in Figure 20.

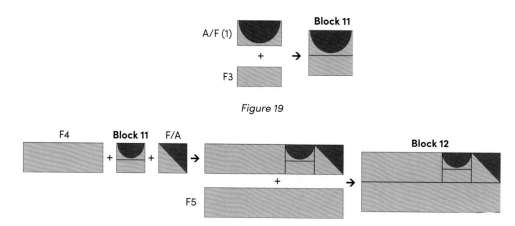

Figure 19

Figure 20

9) To make Block 13, first piece together F/A + A/F (right) + F6 + F/H, then A/F + F6 + F/H (right) + H/I. Next, piece these rows together, as shown in Figure 21.

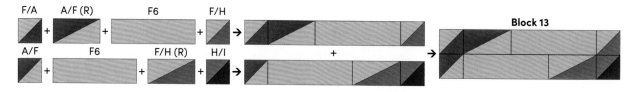

Figure 21

10) To make Row 4, piece together Block 12 + A4 + Block 13, as shown in Figure 22.

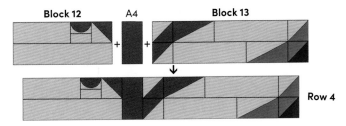

Figure 22

11) To make Block 14, first piece together H/G (left) + G3; I/H + H3 + H/G + G4; then I3 + I/H (left) + H/G (left). Next, piece these rows together, aligning on the left, as shown in Figure 23. Trim excess fabric from the right side of Block 14.

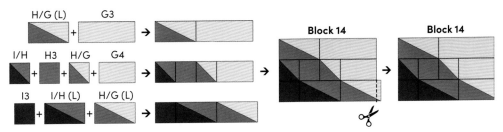

Figure 23

12) To make Block 15, first piece together G5 + G/H (right) + H/I (right) + I4; G6 + G/H + H/I + I5; and G/H (right) + H/I + I6. Next, piece these rows together, aligning on the right, as shown in Figure 24. Trim excess fabric from the left side of Block 15.

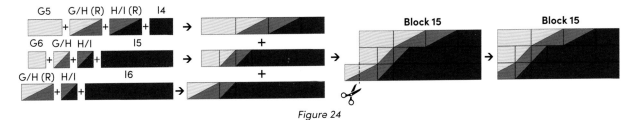

Figure 24

13) To make Row 5, piece together Block 14 + A5 + Block 15, as shown in Figure 25.

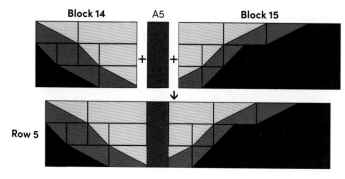

Figure 25

14) Piece together B1 + Rows 1–5, as shown in Figure 26.

Figure 26

To back and quilt your Joshua Tree throw, see Assembling Your Quilt (p. 23).

Joshua Tree Quilt Pattern

Badlands

SOUTH DAKOTA

Badlands National Park in South Dakota was given its name by the Lakota, who called it *mako sica,* which means "land that is bad." Lack of water, steep canyons, jagged cliffs, extreme temperatures, and the land's unsuitability for settlement and farming all contributed to this name. The Badlands were formed over millions of years by rock layers that were stacked on top of each other by natural forces; then, erosion from the Cheyenne River and White River created narrow channels, canyons, and peaks. Within its 240,000 acres you can hike 60 miles of trails, see exhibits of fossils found in the park, and discover more than 400 plant species. Using curves of reds, oranges, and golds to recreate the colorful layered rock formations, this bed quilt captures the dramatic landscapes found in this inhospitable but beautiful place.

Finished Measurements | Height: 106 in. (269.25 cm) Width: 94 in. (238.75 cm)

FABRIC: Art Gallery Fabrics *Pure Solids*, 100% cotton
(width: 44 in. [111.75 cm], weight per yard: 4.7 oz)

A (Turmeric) – 1 yard

B (Grapefruit) – 1 yard

C (Terracotta Tile) – .5 yard

D (Chocolate) – .625 yard

E (Candied Cherry) – .625 yard

F (Cabernet) – .625 yard

G (Blossomed) – 1.875 yards

H (Sweet Macadamia) – 3.25 yards

I (Dried Carrot) – .875 yard

BACKING: Any desired fabric – 8.5 yards

BINDING: Any desired fabric – .875 yard

NOTIONS: Batting – 102 in. x 114 in. (259 cm x 289.5 cm)

TEMPLATES: Badlands 1A, Badlands 1B, Badlands 2A, Badlands 2B

Cutting Instructions | BED QUILT

Note: For more information on cutting and assembling blocks, see p. 14.

A (Turmeric)

Cut three 10.5 in. (26.7 cm) x WOF strips. Subcut:

1 - 10.5 in. x 24.5 in. (26.7 cm x 62.2 cm) [A1]

2 - Template 1A

Sew two strips together, then subcut:

1 - 10.5 in. x 60.5 in. (26.7 cm x 153.7 cm) [A2]

B (Grapefruit)

Cut three 10.5 in. (26.7 cm) x WOF strips. Subcut:

1 - 10.5 in. x 30.5 in. (26.7 cm x 77.5 cm) [B1]

Sew two strips together, then subcut:

1 - 10.5 in. x 66.5 in. (26.7 cm x 169 cm) [B2]

2 - Template 1A

C (Terracotta Tile)

Cut one 10.5 in. (26.7 cm) x WOF strip. Subcut:

1 - 10.5 in. x 36.5 in. (26.7 cm x 92.7 cm) [C1]

Cut one 6 in. (15.2 cm) x WOF strip. Subcut:

1 - Template 1A

D (Chocolate)

Cut two 10.5 in. (26.7 cm) x WOF strips. Sew together, then subcut:

1 - 10.5 in. x 42.5 in. (26.7 cm x 107.9 cm) [D1]

1 - Template 1A

E (Candied Cherry)

Cut two 10.5 in. (26.7 cm) x WOF strips. Sew together, then subcut:

1 - 10.5 in. x 48.5 in. (26.7 cm x 123.2 cm) [E1]

1 - Template 1A

F (Cabernet)

Cut two 10.5 in. (26.7 cm) x WOF strips. Sew together, then subcut:

1 - 10.5 in. x 54.5 in. (26.7 cm x 138.4 cm) [F1]

1 - Template 1A

G (Blossomed)

Cut two 14.5 in. (36.8 cm) x WOF strips. Sew together, then subcut:

1 - 14.5 in. x 52.5 in. (36.8 cm x 133.3 cm) [G1]

1 - 14.5 in. x 28.5 in. (36.8 cm x 72.4 cm) [G2]

Cut two 10.5 in. (26.7 cm)
x WOF strips. Sew together,
then subcut:

   1 - 10.5 in. x 80.5 in.
   (26.7 cm x 204.5 cm) [G3]

Cut one 15.75 in. (40 cm)
x WOF strip. Subcut:

   1 - Template 2B

☐ **H** (Sweet Macadamia)

Cut one 2.5 in. (6.3 cm)
x WOF strip. Subcut:

   2 - 2.5 in. x 14.5 in.
   (36.8 cm) [H9]

Cut five 10.5 in. (26.7 cm)
x WOF strips. Sew together,
then subcut:

   1 - 10.5 in. x 36.5 in.
   (26.7 cm x 92.7 cm) [H1]
   1 - 10.5 in. x 30.5 in.
   (26.7 cm x 77.5 cm) [H2]
   1 - 10.5 in. x 24.5 in.
   (26.7 cm x 62.2 cm) [H3]
   1 - 10.5 in. x 32.5 in.
   (26.7 cm x 82.5 cm) [H4]
   1 - 10.5 in. x 26.5 in.
   (26.7 cm x 67.5 cm) [H5]
   1 - 10.5 in. x 20.5 in.
   (26.7 cm x 52 cm) [H6]
   1 - 10.5 in. x 14.5 in.
   (26.7 cm x 36.8 cm) [H7]
   1 - 8.5 in. x 10.5 in.
   (21.6 cm x 26.7 cm) [H8]

Cut two 16.5 in. (42 cm)
x WOF strips. Sew together,
then subcut:

   1 - 16.5 in. x 80.5 in.
   (42 cm x 204.5 cm) [H10]

Cut two 7 in. (17.8 cm)
x WOF strips. Subcut:

   6 - Template 1B

Cut one 15.75 in. (40 cm)
x WOF strip. Subcut:

   1 - Template 2B
   2 - Template 1B (8 total)

☐ **I** (Dried Carrot)

Cut two 13 in. (33 cm)
x WOF strips. Subcut:

   2 - Template 2A

BINDING Cut eleven 2.5 in.
(6.3 cm) x WOF strips of the
binding fabric.

Block Assembly

1) The Badlands National Park quilt uses half-curve templates (1A, 1B, 2A, and 2B). See Half-Curves (p. 14) for half-curve piecing and trimming instructions. Refer to Figures 1 and 2 to determine the required amount and fabric combinations of the Template Blocks. Trim Template Block 1 to 6.5 in. x 10.5 in. (16.5 cm x 26.7 cm) and Template Block 2 to 14.5 in. x 26.5 in. (36.8 cm x 67.3 cm).

TEMPLATE BLOCK 1

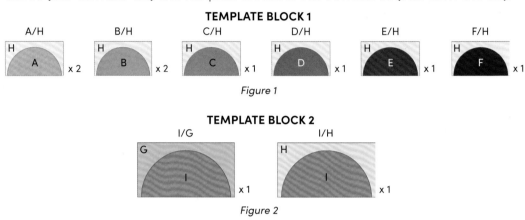

Figure 1

TEMPLATE BLOCK 2

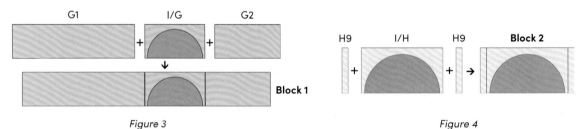

Figure 2

Quilt Assembly

1) To make Block 1, piece together G1 + I/G + G2, as shown in Figure 3. To make Block 2, piece together H9 + I/H + H9, as shown in Figure 4.

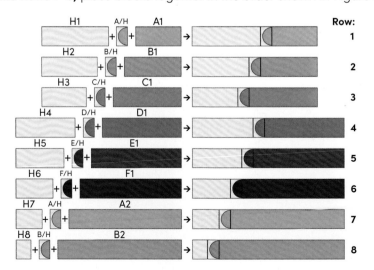

Figure 3

Figure 4

2) To make Rows 1–8, piece blocks together in the order shown in Figure 5.

Figure 5

3) To make Block 3, piece together Rows 1–3, as shown in Figure 6.
To make Block 4, piece together Block 2 + Block 3, as shown in Figure 7.

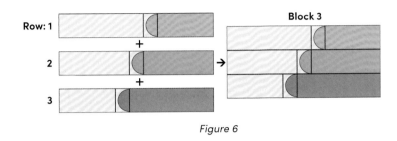

Figure 6

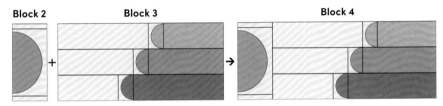

Figure 7

4) To make Block 5, piece together G3 + H10 + Block 4 + Rows 4–8, as shown in Figure 8.

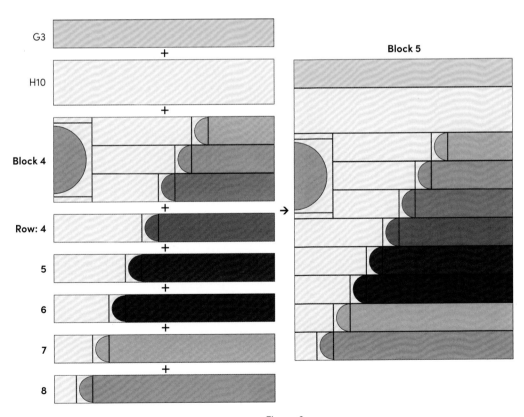

Figure 8

5) Piece together Block 1 + Block 5, as shown in Figure 9.

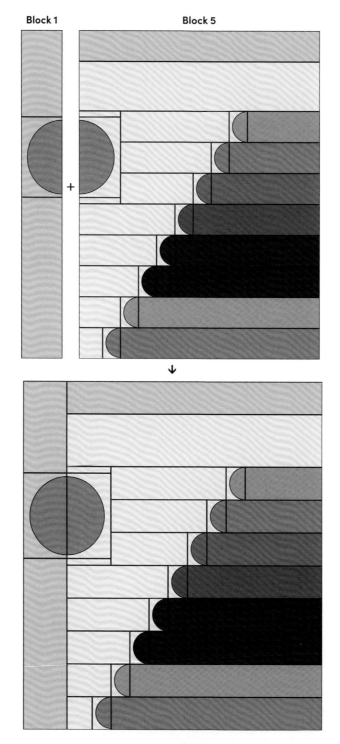

Figure 9

To back and quilt your Badlands bed quilt, see Assembling Your Quilt (p. 23).

Badlands Quilt Pattern

Olympic

WASHINGTON

Located on the Olympic Peninsula in Washington on nearly one million acres, Olympic National Park has a bit of everything: glacier-capped mountains, a temperate rainforest that is home to 1,000-year-old trees reaching up to 300 feet tall and that receives more than 12 feet of rain per year, waterfalls, hot springs, and 70 miles of rocky Pacific coastline. The park also contains an estimated 266 glaciers and more than 3,000 miles of rivers and streams. Using half-rectangle triangles and half-square triangles, this bed quilt captures the reflection of the jagged mountain peaks surrounding the deep, clear blue water of Lake Crescent. Formed by glaciers, the lake has a depth of 624 feet, one of the deepest in the United States, and you can see as far down as 60 feet in some areas.

Finished Measurements | Height: 98 in. (248.9 cm) Width: 91 in. (231.1 cm)

FABRIC: Art Gallery Fabrics *Pure Solids*, 100% cotton
(width: 44 in. [111.75 cm], weight per yard: 4.7 oz)

■ **A** (Evergreen) – 1.125 yards

■ **B** (Mediterraneo) – .75 yard

■ **C** (Parisian Blue) – 2 yards

■ **D** (Aero Blue) – 1 yard

■ **E** (Tranquil Waters) – 1 yard

□ **F** (Periwinkle) – 3.625 yards

BACKING: Any desired
fabric – 8.25 yards

BINDING: Any desired
fabric – .75 yard

NOTIONS: Batting – 99 in. x
106 in. (251.4 cm x 269.2 cm)

Cutting Instructions | BED QUILT

Note: For more information on cutting and assembling blocks, see p. 14.

■ A (Evergreen)

*Cut one 8.5 in. (21.6 cm)
x WOF strip. Subcut:*

> **6** - 4.25 in. x 8.5 in.
> (10.8 cm x 21.6 cm) [A1]
> **2** - 4.25 in. x 4.25 in.
> (10.8 cm x 10.8 cm) [A2]
> **2** - 3.75 in. x 3.75 in.
> (9.5 cm x 9.5 cm) [A3]

*Cut eight 3.75 in. (9.5 cm)
x WOF strips. Subcut:*

one strip:

> **1** - 3.75 in. x 23.25 in.
> (9.5 cm x 59 cm) [A6]
> **1** - 3.75 in. x 16.75 in.
> (9.5 cm x 42.5 cm) [A5]

one strip:

> **1** - 3.75 in. x 23.25 in.
> (9.5 cm x 59 cm)
> [A6 – 2 total]
> **1** - 3.75 in. x 16.75 in.
> (9.5 cm x 42.5 cm)
> [A5 – 2 total]

remaining strips:

> **2** - 3.75 in. x 39.5 in.
> (9.5 cm x 100.3 cm) [A9]
> **2** - 3.75 in. x 33 in.
> (9.5 cm x 81.3 cm) [A8]
> **2** - 3.75 in. x 29.75 in.
> (9.5 cm x 75.5 cm) [A7]
> **2** - 3.75 in. x 10.25 in.
> (9.5 cm x 26 cm) [A4]

■ B (Mediterraneo)

*Cut one 8.5 in. (21.6 cm)
x WOF strip. Subcut:*

> **9** - 4.25 in. x 8.5 in.
> (10.8 cm x 21.6 cm) [B1]

*Cut one 4.25 in. (10.8 cm)
x WOF strip. Subcut:*

> **1** - 4.25 in. x 8.5 in.
> (10.8 cm x 21.6 cm)
> [B1 – 10 total]
> **3** - 4.25 in. x 4.25 in.
> (10.8 cm x 10.8 cm) [B2]
> **1** - 3.75 in. x 10.25 in.
> (9.5 cm x 26 cm) [B3]

*Cut three 3.75 in. (9.5 cm)
x WOF strips. Subcut:*

> **8** - 3.75 in. x 13.5 in.
> (9.5 cm x 34.3 cm) [B4]
> **1** - 3.75 in. x 10.25 in.
> (9.5 cm x 26 cm) [B3 – 2 total]

■ C (Parisian Blue)

*Cut two 8.5 in. (21.6 cm)
x WOF strips. Subcut:*

one strip:

> **9** - 4.25 in. x 8.5 in.
> (10.8 cm x 21.6 cm) [C1]
> **1** - 3.75 in. x 8.25 in.
> (9.5 cm x 21 cm) [C4]

one strip:

> **7** - 4.25 in. x 8.5 in.
> (10.8 cm x 21.6 cm)
> [C1 – 16 total]
> **4** - 4.25 in. x 4.25 in.
> (10.8 cm x 10.8 cm) [C2]
> **1** - 3.75 in. x 8.25 in.
> (9.5 cm x 21 cm)
> [C4 – 2 total]

Cut one 4.25 in. (10.8 cm)
x WOF strip. Subcut:

> **3** - 4.25 in. x 4.25 in.
> (10.8 cm x 10.8 cm)
> [C2 – 7 total]
>
> **2** - 3.75 in. x 11.5 in.
> (9.5 cm x 29.2 cm) [C5]
>
> **2** - 1.75 in. x 3.75 in.
> (4.4 cm x 9.5 cm) [C3]

Cut eleven 3.75 in. (9.5 cm)
x WOF strips. Sew five strips
together, then subcut:

> **4** - 3.75 in. x 29.75 in.
> (9.5 cm x 75.5 cm) [C7]
>
> **2** - 3.75 in. x 26.5 in.
> (9.5 cm x 67.3 cm) [C8]

one strip:

> **1** - 3.75 in. x 13.5 in.
> (9.5 cm x 34.3 cm) [C9]
>
> **1** - 3.75 in. x 23.25 in.
> (9.5 cm x 59 cm) [C10]

one strip:

> **1** - 3.75 in. x 13.5 in.
> (9.5 cm x 34.3 cm) [C9]
>
> **1** - 3.75 in. x 23.25 in.
> (9.5 cm x 59 cm) [C10]

one strip:

> **1** - 3.75 in. x 13.5 in.
> (9.5 cm x 34.3 cm) [C9]
>
> **1** - 3.75 in. x 23.25 in.
> (9.5 cm x 59 cm) [C10]

one strip:

> **1** - 3.75 in. x 13.5 in.
> (9.5 cm x 34.3 cm)
> [C9 – 4 total]
>
> **1** - 3.75 in. x 23.25 in.
> (9.5 cm x 59 cm)
> [C10 – 4 total]

two remaining strips:

> **4** - 3.75 in. x 20 in.
> (9.5 cm x 50.8 cm) [C6]

D (Aero Blue)

Cut one 10.5 in. (26.7 cm)
x WOF strip. Subcut:

> **2** - 5.25 in. x 10.5 in.
> (13.3 cm x 26.7 cm) [D3]
>
> **6** - 4.25 in. x 8.5 in.
> (10.8 cm x 21.6 cm) [D1]
>
> **2** - 4.25 in. x 4.25 in.
> (10.8 cm x 10.8 cm) [D2]

Cut six 3.75 in. (9.5 cm)
x WOF strips. Subcut:

one strip:

> **1** - 3.75 in. x 26.5 in.
> (9.5 cm x 67.3 cm) [D8]
>
> **1** - 3.75 in. x 13.5 in.
> (9.5 cm x 34.3 cm) [D6]

one strip:

> **1** - 3.75 in. x 26.5 in.
> (9.5 cm x 67.3 cm)
> [D8 – 2 total]
>
> **1** - 3.75 in. x 13.5 in.
> (9.5 cm x 34.3 cm)
> [D6 – 2 total]

two strips:

> **4** - 3.75 in. x 20 in.
> (9.5 cm x 50.8 cm) [D7]

one strip:

> **2** - 3.75 in. x 10.25 in.
> (9.5 cm x 26 cm) [D9]
>
> **2** - 3.75 in. x 7 in.
> (9.5 cm x 17.8 cm) [D5]

one strip:

> **6** - 3.75 in. x 3.75 in.
> (9.5 cm x 9.5 cm) [D4]

E (Tranquil Waters)

Cut one 10.5 in. (26.7 cm)
x WOF strip. Subcut:

> **2** - 5.25 in. x 10.5 in.
> (13.3 cm x 26.7 cm) [E3]
>
> **5** - 4.25 in. x 8.5 in.
> (10.8 cm x 21.6 cm) [E1]

Cut one 8.5 in. (21.6 cm)
x WOF strip. Subcut:

> **9** - 4.25 in. x 8.5 in.
> (10.8 cm x 21.6 cm)
> [E1 – 14 total]

Cut three 3.75 in. (9.5 cm)
x WOF strips. Subcut:

one strip:

> **2** - 3.75 in. x 16.75 in.
> (9.5 cm x 42.5 cm) [E7]
>
> **2** - 3.75 in. x 3.75 in.
> (9.5 cm x 9.5 cm) [E5]

one strip:

> **4** - 3.75 in. x 10.25 in.
> (9.5 cm x 26 cm) [E4]

one strip:

> **2** - 3.75 in. x 10.25 in.
> (9.5 cm x 26 cm)
> [E4 – 6 total]
>
> **3** - 3.75 in. x 7 in.
> (9.5 cm x 17.8 cm) [E6]

Cut one 4.25 in. (10.8 cm)
x WOF strip. Subcut:

> **5** - 4.25 in. x 4.25 in.
> (10.8 cm x 10.8 cm) [E2]
>
> **1** - 3.75 in. x 7 in.
> (9.5 cm x 17.8 cm)
> [E6 – 4 total]

F (Periwinkle)

Cut one 8.5 in. (21.6 cm)
x WOF strip. Subcut:

> **8** - 4.25 in. x 8.5 in.
> (10.8 cm x 21.6 cm) [F1]
>
> **4** - 3.75 in. x 3.75 in.
> (9.5 cm x 9.5 cm) [F5]

Continued on next page

Cut one 4.25 in. (10.8 cm) x WOF strip. Subcut:

7 – 4.25 in. x 4.25 in. (10.8 cm x 10.8 cm) [F2]

2 – 3.75 in. x 3.75 in. (9.5 cm x 9.5 cm) [F5 – 6 total]

Cut thirteen 3.75 in. (9.5 cm) x WOF strips. Subcut:

one strip:

1 – 3.75 in. x 16.75 in. (9.5 cm x 42.5 cm) [F8]

1 – 3.75 in. x 23.25 in. (9.5 cm x 59 cm) [F7]

one strip:

1 – 3.75 in. x 16.75 in. (9.5 cm x 42.5 cm) [F8 – 2 total]

1 – 3.75 in. x 23.25 in. (9.5 cm x 59 cm) [F7 – 2 total]

Sew eleven strips together, then subcut:

2 – 3.75 in. x 61 in. (9.5 cm x 155 cm) [F6]

2 – 3.75 in. x 80.5 in. (9.5 cm x 204.5 cm) [F4]

2 – 3.75 in. x 83.75 in. (9.5 cm x 212.7 cm) [F3]

Cut twenty-nine 1.75 in. (4.4 cm) x WOF strips. Sew together, then subcut:

13 – 1.75 in. x 91.5 in. (4.4 cm x 232.4 cm) [F9]

Cut three 4.25 in. (10.8 cm) x WOF strips. Subcut:

1 – 4.25 in. x 91.5 in. (10.8 cm x 232.4 cm) [F10]

BINDING Cut ten 2.5 in. (6.3 cm) x WOF strips of the binding fabric.

Block Assembly

1) HRTs are sewn in two different orientations (right and left). Organize each A1, B1, C1, D1, E1, F1, D3, and E3 rectangle into piles, referring to Figure 1 to determine the required amount for each right/left orientation. Cut each rectangle in half diagonally, paying close attention to the direction each is cut. Keep each HRT in its right/left orientation stack.

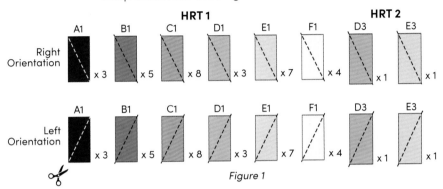

Figure 1

2) Pair each cut triangle with its corresponding cut triangle, as shown in Figure 2. Refer to Figure 2 to determine the required amount and fabric combinations of HRTs. See Half-Rectangle Triangles (p. 16) for HRT piecing and trimming instructions. Trim HRT 1 to 3.75 in. x 7 in. (9.5 cm x 17.8 cm) and HRT 2 to 4.25 in. x 8.5 in. (10.8 cm x 21.6 cm).

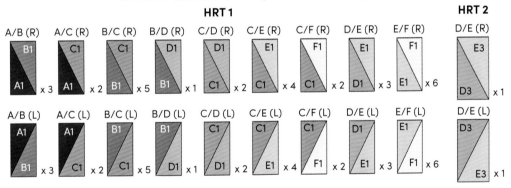

Figure 2

3) To make HRT 3, cut the required amount of trimmed HRT 2 blocks in half on the diagonal noting each orientation, as shown in Figure 3. Discard the triangle with the red X and align each HRT 2 triangle with the remaining C1 triangles. Make two HRT 3 blocks, one HRT 3 (left) and one HRT 3 (right). Trim HRT 3 to 3.75 in. x 7 in. (9.5 cm x 17.8 cm).

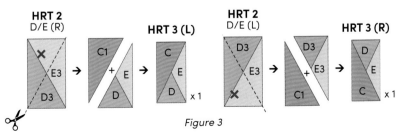

Figure 3

4) To make the HSTs, pair each A2, B2, C2, D2, E2, and F2 square with its corresponding square, as shown in Figure 4. Refer to Figure 4 to determine the required amount and fabric combinations of HSTs. See Half-Square Triangles (p. 19) for two-at-a-time HST piecing and trimming instructions. Trim HSTs to 3.75 in. x 3.75 in. (9.5 cm x 9.5 cm).

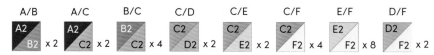

Figure 4

5) After trimming the HSTs, take two E/F HSTs and pair each with a D4 square. Place D4 on top of an E/F HST and draw a diagonal line through the block, perpendicular to the E/F seam, as shown in Figure 5. Sew directly on the marked center line. Trim a .25 in. (.6 cm) seam allowance on the dotted line toward the side of the HST with the red X and press the seams open. Discard the trimmed piece. Make two HST 2 blocks, one HST 2A and one HST 2B. HST 2 blocks are mirrored, so pay close attention to the orientation of each E/F HST prior to placing D4 and sewing.

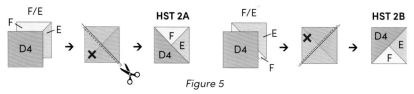

Figure 5

Quilt Assembly

1) To make Rows 1–12, piece blocks together in the order shown in Figure 6. Row 11 will be longer than the other rows.

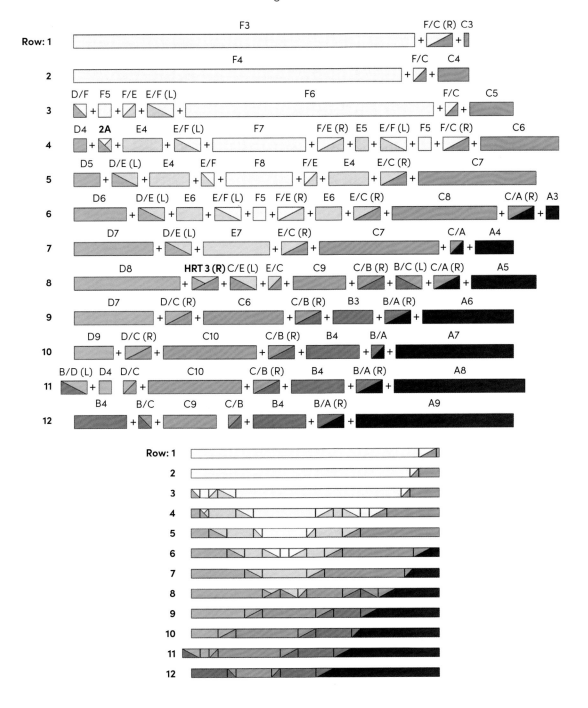

Figure 6

2) To make Rows 13–24, piece blocks together in the order shown in Figure 7. Row 14 will be longer than the other rows.

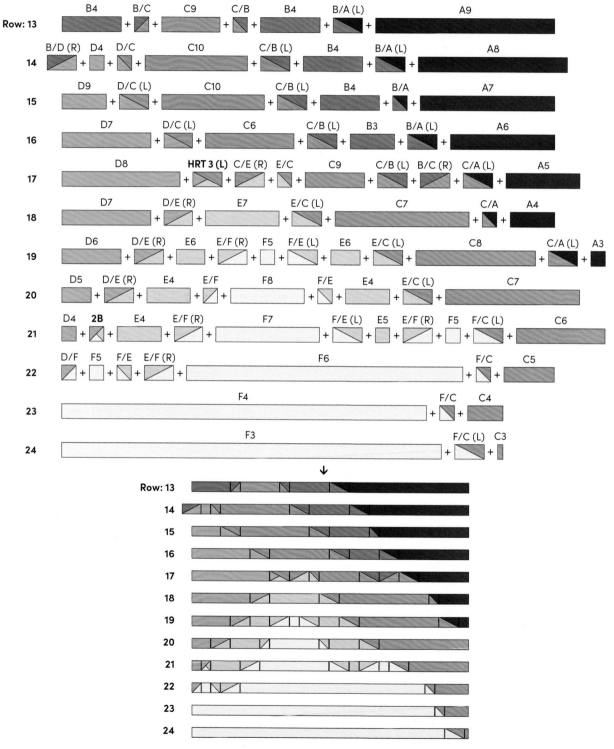

Figure 7

3) To make Block 1, piece together F9 + Rows 1–12, as shown in Figure 8. Align the rows on the right side, with Row 11 extending to the left.

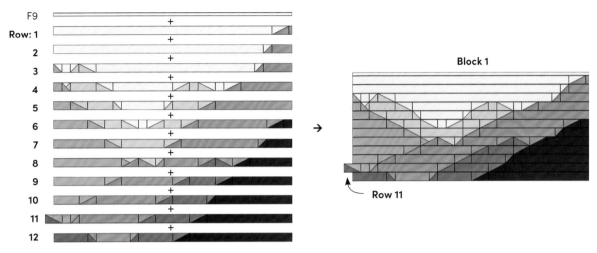

Figure 8

4) To make Block 2, piece together Rows 13–24 with an F9 strip on top and between each row, and F10 at the bottom, as shown in Figure 9. Align the rows on the right side, with Row 14 extending to the left.

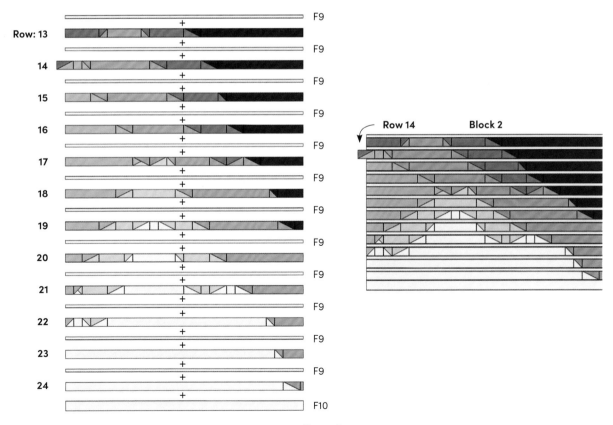

Figure 9

5) Trim excess fabric from Block 1 (Row 11) and Block 2 (Row 14), as shown in Figure 10.

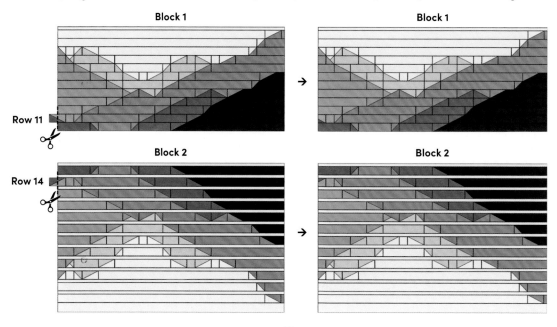

Figure 10

6) Piece together Block 1 + Block 2, as shown in Figure 11.

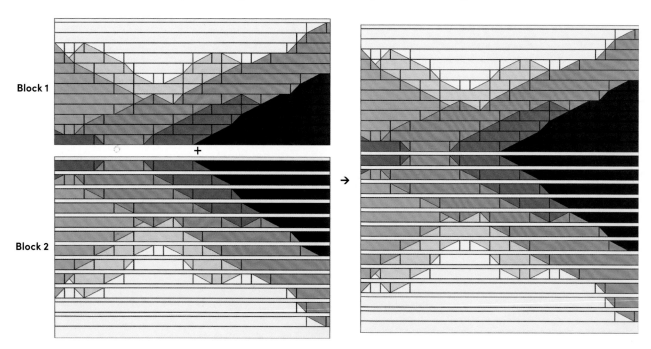

Figure 11

To back and quilt your Olympic bed quilt, see Assembling Your Quilt (p. 23).

Olympic Quilt Pattern

Great Smoky Mountains

NORTH CAROLINA / TENNESSEE

Straddling the border of North Carolina and Tennessee, Great Smoky Mountains National Park covers more than 500,000 acres of lush forests, streams, rivers, waterfalls, and ancient mountains. Thought to be between 200 and 300 million years old, these are the oldest mountain ranges on Earth. The Cherokee refer to this area as Shaconage, which means "Land of Blue Smoke." The "smoky" appearance comes from a blue-colored fog created by the park's millions of plants as their vapor molecules scatter blue light from the sky. The park contains 800 miles of trails, 2,900 miles of fishable streams, and 30 salamander species, making it the Salamander Capital of the World. This bed quilt uses half-rectangle triangles and eight fabrics ranging from deep blues to soft purples to capture the hazy colors of the Great Smoky Mountains.

Finished Measurements | Height: 90 in. (228.6 cm) Width: 90 in. (228.6 cm)

FABRIC: Art Gallery Fabrics *Pure Solids*, 100% cotton
(width: 44 in. [111.75 cm], weight per yard: 4.7 oz)

A (Cotton Candy) – 1.5 yards

B (Field of Lavender) – .75 yard

C (Wisteria) – 1 yard

D (Amethyst) – 1 yard

E (Atmospheric) – .75 yard

F (Aero Blue) – 1.25 yards

G (Parisian Blue) – .875 yard

H (Heart of the Ocean) – 1.875 yards

BACKING: Any desired fabric – 8.25 yards

BINDING: Any desired fabric – .75 yard

NOTIONS: Batting – 98 in. x 98 in. (249 cm x 249 cm)

Cutting Instructions | BED QUILT

Note: For more information on cutting and assembling blocks, see p. 14.

A (Cotton Candy)

Cut one 5.5 in. (14 cm) x WOF strip. Subcut:

1 - 5.5 in. x 9.25 in. (14 cm x 23.5 cm) [A8]

2 - 1.75 in. x 5.5 in. (4.4 cm x 14 cm) [A4]

2 - 3.5 in. x 7 in. (8.9 cm x 17.8 cm) [A2]

2 - 1.75 in. x 11.75 in. (4.4 cm x 29.8 cm) [A3]

Cut one 4.25 in. (10.8 cm) x WOF strip. Subcut:

1 - 4.25 in. x 23 in. (10.8 cm x 58.4 cm) [A9]

1 - 2.25 in. x 4.25 in. (5.7 cm x 10.8 cm) [A5]

1 - 2.5 in. x 4.25 in. (6.3 cm x 10.8 cm) [A6]

1 - 3 in. x 4.25 in. (7.6 cm x 10.8 cm) [A7]

Cut three 13 in. (33 cm) x WOF strips. Sew together, then subcut:

1 - 13 in. x 90.5 in. (33 cm x 230 cm) [A10]

4 - 5.5 in. x 14 in. (14 cm x 35.5 cm) [A1]

B (Field of Lavender)

Cut two 5.5 in. (14 cm) x WOF strips. Subcut:

6 - 5.5 in. x 14 in. (14 cm x 35.5 cm) [B1]

Cut one 3.5 in. (8.9 cm) x WOF strip. Subcut:

4 - 3.5 in. x 7 in. (8.9 cm x 17.8 cm) [B2]

Cut two 3 in. (7.6 cm) x WOF strips. Subcut:

2 - 3 in. x 11.75 in. (7.6 cm x 29.8 cm) [B3]

1 - 3 in. x 35.5 in. (7.6 cm x 90.2 cm) [B5]

Cut one 4.25 in. (10.8 cm) x WOF strip. Subcut:

1 - 4.25 in. x 36.75 in. (10.8 cm x 93.3 cm) [B4]

C (Wisteria)

Cut two 5.5 in. (14 cm) x WOF strips. Subcut:

6 - 5.5 in. x 14 in. (14 cm x 35.5 cm) [C1]

Cut one 6.25 in. (15.9 cm) x WOF strip. Subcut:

1 - 6.25 in. x 8 in. (15.9 cm x 20.3 cm) [C7]

1 - 5.5 in. x 14 in. (14 cm x 35.5 cm) [C1 – 7 total]

1 - 1.75 in. x 5.5 in. (4.4 cm x 14 cm) [C3]

1 - 5 in. x 9.5 in. (12.7 cm x 24 cm) [C4]

Cut one 5 in. (12.7 cm) x WOF strip. Sew together with C4 piece above, then subcut:

1 - 5 in. x 50.5 in. (12.7 cm x 128.2 cm) [C4]

Cut one 4.25 in. (10.8 cm) x WOF strip. Subcut:

1 - 4.25 in. x 23 in. (10.8 cm x 58.4 cm) [C8]

1 - 4.25 in. x 11.75 in. (10.8 cm x 29.8 cm) [C9]

Cut one 3.75 in. (9.5 cm) x WOF strip. Subcut:

1 - 3.75 in. x 10.5 in. (9.5 cm x 26.7 cm) [C6]

4 - 3.5 in. x 7 in. (8.9 cm x 17.8 cm) [C2]

1 - 1.75 in. x 3 in. (4.4 cm x 7.6 cm) [C10]

Cut one 2.5 in. (6.3 cm) x WOF strip. Subcut:

1 - 2.5 in. x 23 in. (6.3 cm x 58.4 cm) [C5]

D (Amethyst)

Cut two 5.5 in. (14 cm) x WOF strips. Subcut:

5 - 5.5 in. x 14 in. (14 cm x 35.5 cm) [D1]

1 - 3.5 in. x 7 in. (8.9 cm x 17.8 cm) [D2]

1 - 1.75 in. x 11.75 in. (4.4 cm x 29.8 cm) [D3]

Cut one 3.5 in. (8.9 cm) x WOF strip. Subcut:

6 - 3.5 in. x 7 in. (8.9 cm x 17.8 cm) [D2 – 7 total]

Cut two 4.25 in. (10.8 cm) x WOF strips. Sew together, then subcut:

1 - 4.25 in. x 34.25 in. (10.8 cm x 87 cm) [D4]

1 - 4.25 in. x 23 in. (10.8 cm x 58.4 cm) [D5]

1 - 4.25 in. x 20.5 in. (10.8 cm x 52 cm) [D9]

1 - 4.25 in. x 4.75 in. (10.8 cm x 12 cm) [D8]

Cut three 3.25 in. (8.2 cm) x WOF strips. Sew together, then subcut:

1 - 3.25 in. x 90.5 in. (8.2 cm x 229.9 cm) [D10]

1 - 3 in. x 7.5 in. (7.6 cm x 19 cm) [D6]

1 - 3 in. x 10.5 in. (7.6 cm x 26.7 cm) [D7]

E (Atmospheric)

Cut three 5.5 in. (14 cm) x WOF strips. Subcut:

1 - 5.5 in. x 38.5 in. (14 cm x 97.8 cm) [E6]

4 - 5.5 in. x 14 in. (14 cm x 35.5 cm) [E1]

1 - 3 in. x 5.5 in. (7.6 cm x 14 cm) [E4]

1 - 4.25 in. x 10 in. (10.8 cm x 25.4 cm) [E5]

1 - 3.5 in. x 4.25 in. (8.9 cm x 10.8 cm) [E7]

1 - 3.5 in. x 7 in. (8.9 cm x 17.8 cm) [E2]

Cut one 3.5 in. (8.9 cm) x WOF strip. Subcut:

6 - 3.5 in. x 7 in. (8.9 cm x 17.8 cm) [E2 – 7 total]

Cut one 3 in. (7.6 cm) x WOF strip. Subcut:

1 - 3 in. x 12.5 in. (7.6 cm x 31.7 cm) [E3]

F (Aero Blue)

Cut two 5.5 in. (14 cm) x WOF strips. Subcut:

5 - 5.5 in. x 14 in. (14 cm x 35.5 cm) [F1]

1 - 1.75 in. x 5.5 in. (4.4 cm x 14 cm) [F4]

1 - 3 in. x 10.5 in. (7.6 cm x 26.7 cm) [F3]

1 - 1.75 in. x 10.5 in. (4.4 cm x 26.7 cm) [F5]

Cut one 3.5 in. (8.9 cm) x WOF strip. Subcut:

5 - 3.5 in. x 7 in. (8.9 cm x 17.8 cm) [F2]

Cut three 4.25 in. (10.8 cm) x WOF strips. Sew together, then subcut:

1 - 4.25 in. x 30 in. (10.8 cm x 76.2 cm) [F6]

1 - 4.25 in. x 20.5 in. (10.8 cm x 52 cm) [F7]

2 - 4.25 in. x 5.5 in. (10.8 cm x 14 cm) [F8]

1 - 4.25 in. x 32.75 in. (10.8 cm x 83.2 cm) [F10]

Cut two 6.75 in. (17.1 cm) x WOF strips. Sew together, then subcut:

1 - 6.75 in. x 74.25 in. (17.1 cm x 188.6 cm) [F9]

G (Parisian Blue)

Cut two 5.5 in. (14 cm) x WOF strips. Subcut:

4 - 5.5 in. x 14 in. (14 cm x 35.5 cm) [G1]

1 - 4.25 in. x 25.5 in. (10.8 cm x 64.8 cm) [G6]

Continued on next page

Cut one 4.25 in. (10.8 cm)
x WOF strip. Subcut:

> **1** – 4.25 in. x 19.5 in.
> (10.8 cm x 49.5 cm) [G4]
>
> **1** – 4.25 in. x 14.25 in.
> (10.8 cm x 36.2 cm) [G7]
>
> **1** – 3.5 in. x 7 in.
> (8.9 cm x 17.8 cm) [G2]

Cut one 3 in. (7.6 cm)
x WOF strip. Subcut:

> **1** – 3 in. x 11.75 in.
> (7.6 cm x 29.8 cm) [G3]

Cut one 8 in. (20.3 cm)
x WOF strip. Subcut:

> **1** – 8 in. x 40.5 in.
> (20.3 cm x 102.9 cm) [G5]

 **H** (Heart of the Ocean)

Cut one 11 in. (28 cm)
x WOF strip. Subcut:

> **4** – 5.5 in. x 14 in.
> (14 cm x 35.5 cm) [H1]
>
> **1** – 1.75 in. x 5.5 in.
> (4.4 cm x 14 cm) [H3]
>
> **1** – 8 in. x 10.75 in.
> (20.3 cm x 27.3 cm) [H9]

Cut two 10.75 in. (27.3 cm)
x WOF strips. Sew together with
H9 piece above, then subcut:

> **1** – 10.75 in. x 90.5 in.
> (27.3 cm x 229.9 cm) [H9]

Cut seven 4.25 in. (10.8 cm)
x WOF strips. Sew together,
then subcut:

> **1** – 4.25 in. x 23 in.
> (10.8 cm x 58.4 cm) [H4]
>
> **1** – 4.25 in. x 39.25 in.
> (10.8 cm x 99.7 cm) [H5]
>
> **1** – 4.25 in. x 54.25 in.
> (10.8 cm x 137.8 cm) [H6]
>
> **1** – 4.25 in. x 65.5 in.
> (10.8 cm x 166.3 cm) [H7]
>
> **1** – 4.25 in. x 79.25 in.
> (10.8 cm x 201.3 cm) [H8]
>
> **1** – 3.5 in. x 7 in.
> (8.9 cm x 17.8 cm) [H2]

BINDING Cut nine 2.5 in.
(6.3 cm) x WOF strips of the
binding fabric.

Block Assembly

1) HRTs are sewn in two different orientations (right and left). Organize each A1, B1, C1, D1, E1, F1, G1, H1, A2, B2, C2, D2, E2, F2, G2, and H2 rectangle into piles, referring to Figure 1 to determine the required amount for each right/left orientation. Cut each rectangle in half diagonally, paying close attention to the direction each is cut. Keep each HRT in its right/left orientation stack.

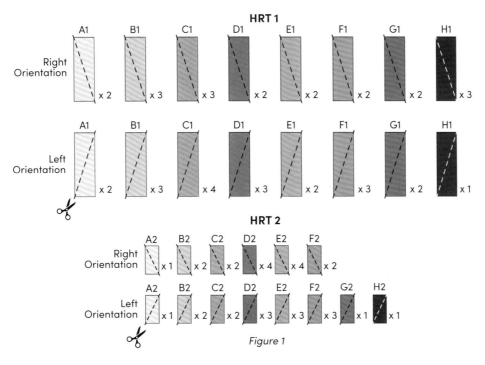

Figure 1

2) Pair each cut triangle with its corresponding cut triangle, as shown in Figure 2. Refer to Figure 2 to determine the required amount and fabric combinations of the HRTs. See Half-Rectangle Triangles (p. 16) for HRT piecing and trimming instructions. Trim HRT 1 to 4.25 in. x 11.75 in. (10.8 cm x 29.8 cm) and HRT 2 to 3 in. x 5.5 in. (7.6 cm x 14 cm).

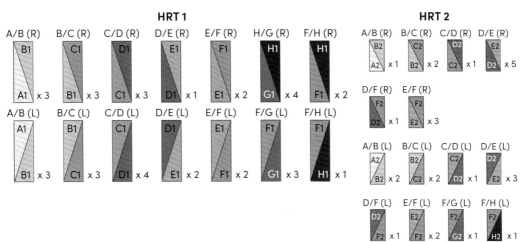

Figure 2

Quilt Assembly

1) To make Block 1, piece together A3 + A/B (HRT 1 – right) + B3, as shown in Figure 3. To make Block 2, piece together A3 + B/A (HRT 1 – left) + B3, as shown in Figure 4.
To make Block 3, piece together A4 + B/A (HRT 2 – left), as shown in Figure 5.

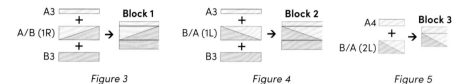

Figure 3   Figure 4   Figure 5

2) To make Block 4, piece together A4 + A/B (HRT 2 – right), as shown in Figure 6.
To make Block 5, piece together Block 3 + A5 + A/B (HRT 1 – right) +
B/A (HRT 1 – left) + A6 + Block 4, as shown in Figure 7.

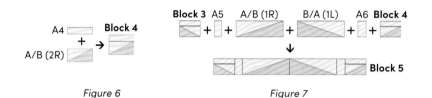

Figure 6   Figure 7

3) To make Block 6, piece together Block 5 + B4, as shown in Figure 8.
To make Block 7, piece together B/A (HRT 2 – left) + A7, as shown in Figure 9.

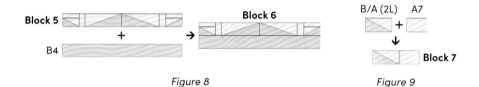

Figure 8   Figure 9

4) To make Block 8, piece together A8 + Block 7, as shown in Figure 10.
To make Block 9, piece together A/B (HRT 1 – right) + B/A (HRT 1 – left), as shown in Figure 11.
To make Block 10, piece together A9 + Block 9, as shown in Figure 12.

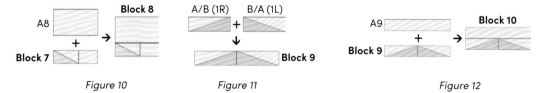

Figure 10   Figure 11   Figure 12

5) To make Row 1, piece together Block 1 + Block 6 + Block 2 + Block 8 + Block 10, as shown in Figure 13.

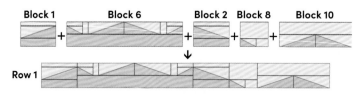

Figure 13

6) To make Block 11, piece together B/C (HRT 2 – right) + C3, as shown in Figure 14.
To make Block 12, piece together Block 11 + C/B (HRT 1 – left) +
B/C (HRT 1 – right) + C/B (HRT 1 – left) + B/C (HRT 1 – right), as shown in Figure 15.

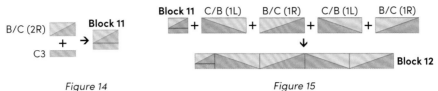

Figure 14   Figure 15

7) To make Block 13, piece together Block 12 + C4, as shown in Figure 16.

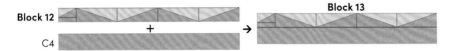

Figure 16

8) To make Block 14, piece together C/B (HRT 2 – left) + B5, as shown in Figure 17.

Figure 17

9) To make Block 15, piece together C/B (HRT 1 – left) + B/C (HRT 1 – right), as shown in Figure 18.
To make Block 16, piece together Block 15 + C5, as shown in Figure 19.

Figure 18   Figure 19

10) To make Block 17, piece together C/B (HRT 2 – left) + B/C (HRT 2 – right), as shown in Figure 20.
To make Block 18, piece together Block 17 + C6, as shown in Figure 21.

Figure 20   Figure 21

11) To make Block 19, piece together C7 + Block 16 + Block 18, as shown in Figure 22.

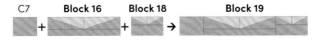

Figure 22

12) To make Block 20, piece together Block 14 + Block 19, as shown in Figure 23.

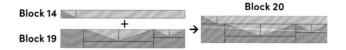

Figure 23

13) To make Row 2, piece together Block 13 + Block 20, as shown in Figure 24.

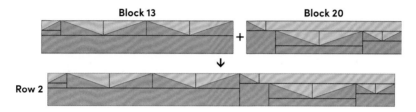

Figure 24

14) To make Row 3, piece together D/C (HRT 1 – left) + C/D (HRT 1 – right) + D/C (HRT 1 – left) + C8 + C/D (HRT 1 – right) + D/C (HRT 1 – left) + C9, as shown in Figure 25.

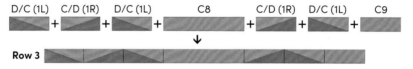

Figure 25

15) To make Block 21, first piece together D/C (HRT 2 – left) + C10 + C/D (HRT 2 – right), then piece D3 to the bottom, as shown in Figure 26.

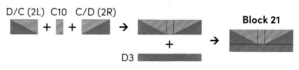

Figure 26

16) To make Row 4, piece together D4 + D/C (HRT 1 – left) + C/D (HRT 1 – right) + D5 + Block 21, as shown in Figure 27.

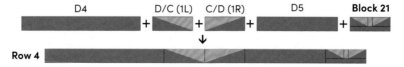

Figure 27

17) To make Block 22, first piece together D6 + D/E (HRT 2 – right) + E/D (HRT 2 – left) + D7 + D/E (HRT 2 – right); D/E (HRT 2 – right) + E3 + E/D (HRT 2 – left) + D/E (HRT 2 – right) + E4; and E5 + E/F (HRT 1 – right) + F/E (HRT 1 – left). Next, piece these rows together, as shown in Figure 28.

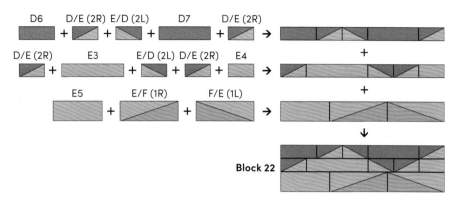

Figure 28

18) To make Block 23, first piece together E/D (HRT 1 – left) + D8 + D/E (HRT 1 – right) + E/D (HRT 1 – left), then piece E6 to the bottom, as shown in Figure 29.

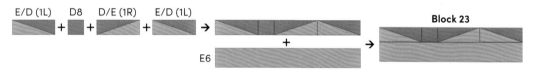

Figure 29

19) To make Block 24, first piece together E/D (HRT 2 – left) + D/F (HRT 2 – right) + F/D (HRT 2 – left) + D/E (HRT 2 – right), and E/F (HRT 2 – right) + F3 + F/E (HRT 2 – left). Next, piece these rows together with D9, as shown in Figure 30.

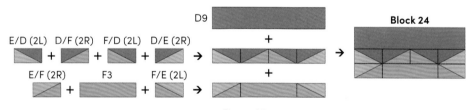

Figure 30

20) To make Row 5, piece together Block 22 + Block 23 + Block 24, as shown in Figure 31.

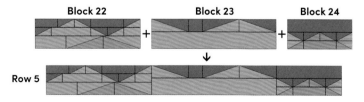

Figure 31

21) To make Block 25, piece together E/F (HRT 2 – right) + F4, as shown in Figure 32. To make Block 26, first piece together F/E (HRT 2 – left) + E/F (HRT 2 – right), then piece F5 to the bottom, as shown in Figure 33.

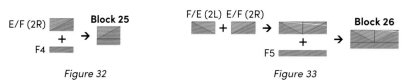

Figure 32   Figure 33

22) To make Row 6, piece together Block 25 + F6 + F/E (HRT 1 – left) + E7 + E/F (HRT 1 – right) + Block 26 + F7, as shown in Figure 34.

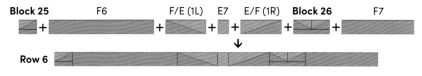

Figure 34

23) To make Block 27, piece together G/F (HRT 1 – left) + G3, as shown in Figure 35. To make Block 28, piece together F8 + G/F (HRT 2 – left), as shown in Figure 36.

Figure 35   Figure 36

24) To make Row 7, piece together Block 27 + Block 28 + F9, as shown in Figure 37.

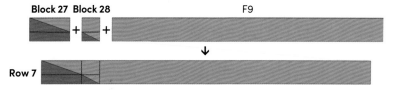

Figure 37

25) To make Row 8, piece together G4 + G/F (HRT 1 – left) + F10 + F/H (HRT 1 – right) + H/F (HRT 1 – left) + F8, as shown in Figure 38.

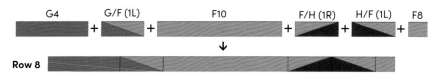

Figure 38

26) To make Block 29, piece together H/F (HRT 2 – left) + H3, as shown in Figure 39.

Figure 39

27) To make Block 30, first piece together G/F (HRT 1 – left) + F/H (HRT 1 – right) + H4 + Block 29, and G/H (HRT 1 – right) + H5. Next, piece these rows together, as shown in Figure 40.

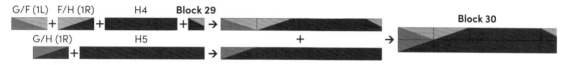

Figure 40

28) To make Row 9, piece together G5 + Block 30, as shown in Figure 41.

Figure 41

29) To make Row 10, piece together G6 + G/H (HRT 1 – right) + H6, as shown in Figure 42.

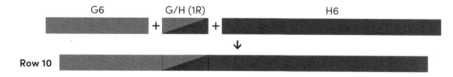

Figure 42

30) To make Row 11, piece together G7 + G/H (HRT 1 – right) + H7, as shown in Figure 43.

Figure 43

31) To make Row 12, piece together G/H (HRT 1 - right) + H8, as shown in Figure 44.

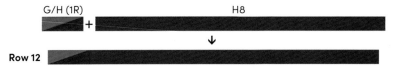

Figure 44

32) Piece together A10 + Rows 1–4 + D10 + Rows 5–12 + H9, as shown in Figure 45.

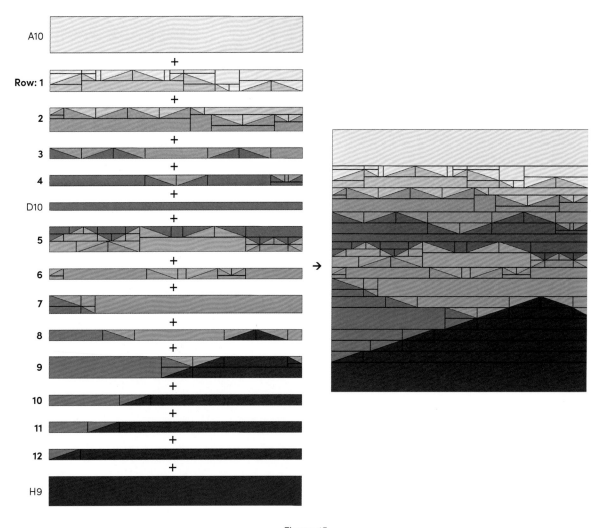

Figure 45

To back and quilt your Great Smoky Mountains bed quilt, see Assembling Your Quilt (p. 23).

Great Smoky Mountains Quilt Pattern

Dry Tortugas
FLORIDA

In the Gulf of Mexico, 70 miles west of Key West, Florida, sits Dry Tortugas National Park on 100 square miles of 99 percent open water. Initially named "Las Islas de Tortugas" after explorers found an abundance of sea turtles, it was later named Dry Tortugas due to the lack of fresh water available on the islands. The beaches continue to be a popular nesting ground for sea turtles. Accessible only by boat or seaplane, the park features shallow waters perfect for snorkeling among protected coral reefs and provides plenty of opportunities for diving, fishing, and camping under the stars on an island out at sea. This bed quilt uses large ombré curves to capture the transition from pristine white sandy beaches to picturesque crystal-clear blue waters to deep sea blues as the ocean depth plunges to more than 600 feet.

Finished Measurements | Height: 87 in. (221 cm) Width: 87 in. (221 cm)

FABRIC: Art Gallery Fabrics *Pure Solids*, 100% cotton
(width: 44 in. [111.75 cm], weight per yard: 4.7 oz)

A (Icy Mint) – .5 yard

B (Fresh Water) – 1 yard

C (Cozumel Blue) – 1 yard

D (Maldives) – 1.33 yards

E (Tile Blue) – 1.875 yards

F (Heart of the Ocean) –
1.875 yards

G (Nocturnal) – 2.625 yards

BACKING: Any desired
fabric – 8 yards

BINDING: Any desired
fabric – .67 yard

NOTIONS: Batting – 95 in. x
95 in. (241.3 cm x 241.3 cm)

TEMPLATES: Dry Tortugas A,
Dry Tortugas B

Cutting Instructions | BED QUILT

Note: For more information on cutting and assembling blocks, see p. 14.

A (Icy Mint)

*Cut one 15.5 in. (39.4 cm)
x WOF strip. Subcut:*

- **1** - Template B
- **1** - Template A
- **1** - 15 in. x 15 in.
(38 cm x 38 cm) [A1]

B (Fresh Water)

*Cut two 15.5 in. (39.4 cm)
x WOF strips. Subcut:*

- **3** - Template B
- **2** - Template A

C (Cozumel Blue)

*Cut two 15.5 in. (39.4 cm)
x WOF strips. Subcut:*

- **3** - Template B
- **4** - Template A

D (Maldives)

*Cut three 15.5 in. (39.4 cm)
x WOF strips. Subcut:*

- **4** - Template B
- **5** - Template A

E (Tile Blue)

*Cut four 15.5 in. (39.4 cm)
x WOF strips. Subcut:*

- **6** - Template B
- **5** - Template A

F (Heart of the Ocean)

*Cut four 15.5 in. (39.4 cm)
x WOF strips. Subcut:*

- **6** - Template B
- **5** - Template A

G (Nocturnal)

*Cut two 15.5 in. (39.4 cm)
x WOF strips. Subcut:*

- **2** - Template B
- **3** - Template A

*Cut four 15 in. (38 cm)
x WOF strips. Sew together,
then subcut:*

- **1** - 15 in. x 15 in.
(38 cm x 38 cm) [G1]
- **1** - 15 in. x 29.5 in.
(38 cm x 75 cm) [G2]
- **1** - 15 in. x 44 in.
(38 cm x 112 cm) [G3]
- **1** - 15 in. x 58.5 in.
(38 cm x 148.5 cm) [G4]

BINDING *Cut nine 2.5 in.
(6.3 cm) x WOF strips of the
binding fabric.*

Block Assembly

1) The Dry Tortugas National Park quilt uses quarter-curve templates (A and B). See Quarter-Curves (p. 15) for quarter-curve piecing and trimming instructions. Refer to Figure 1 to determine the required amount and fabric combinations of the Template Blocks. Trim Template Blocks to 15 in. x 15 in. (38 cm x 38 cm).

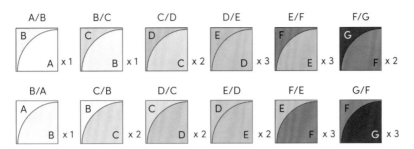

Figure 1

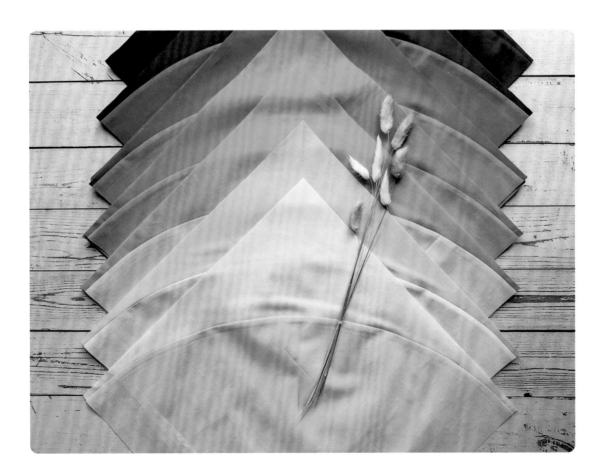

Quilt Assembly

1) To make Rows 1–6, piece blocks together in the order shown in Figure 2.

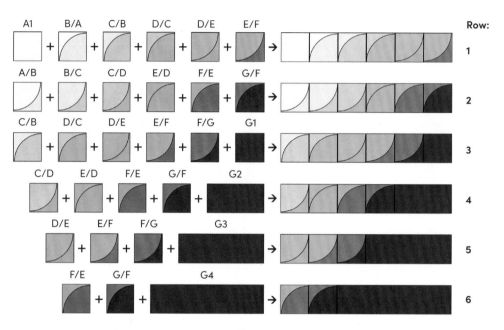

Figure 2

2) Piece together Rows 1–6, as shown in Figure 3.

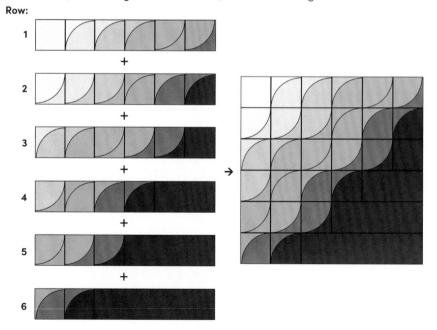

Figure 3

To back and quilt your Dry Tortugas bed quilt, see Assembling Your Quilt (p. 23).

Dry Tortugas Quilt Pattern

Resources

GLOSSARY

BACKING A layer of fabric that covers the batting. Quilt backings should be 4 in. (10.2 cm) larger than your quilt top on all sides.

BASTING Using pins or basting spray to temporarily hold the quilt layers together while quilting.

BATTING The layer of insulation between the quilt top and backing that adds weight and warmth to a quilt. There are various types of batting, including cotton, polyester, cotton blends, wool, silk, and bamboo.

BINDING Used to encase the outer raw edges of a quilt sandwich and prevent fabric from fraying.

BLOCK Created by sewing fabric pieces together to create a specific design.

CHAIN PIECING Sewing multiple blocks together assembly line style without pausing to snip threads or lift your presser foot. A huge time-saver, this method will result in multiple blocks sewn together on one continuous thread.

HERA MARKER A marking tool for quilting that leaves a crease in the fabric for you to follow.

HRT Half-rectangle triangle, made up of two elongated triangles sewn together along their diagonal sides. HRTs are not symmetrical and cannot be interchanged, so the direction of the diagonal cut is very important. The HRTs used in this book's projects have a right or left orientation. Refer to each pattern to determine the required amount of each orientation.

HST Half-square triangle, made up of two right-angle triangles sewn together along their diagonal sides.

LOG CABIN BLOCKS Sewing strips of fabric around a central square.

NESTING SEAMS Pressing the seam allowance to one side for one unit, then in the opposite direction for the second unit, so the fabrics interlock when sewing the two units together.

PANTOGRAPH Used for longarm quilting, a pantograph creates a continuous line design that covers the entire quilt top from edge to edge.

PIECING Sewing fabric together after it has been cut to make a specific block or quilt top.

POINT TURNER A tool used to create crisp and clean corners on your pillow.

PRESSING Using an iron to press seams flat after they have been sewn. Seams can be pressed to the side or open, often according to personal preference.

QUILT SANDWICH The three layers that make up a quilt: the quilt top, batting, and backing.

QUILT TOP A single layer of pieced blocks that result in the finished top and what is seen when the quilt is facing right side up.

QUILTING Stitching the three layers of the quilt together, often using a design or pattern.

RAW EDGE The unfinished edge of the fabric that can result in fraying if not encased in binding.

RIGHT SIDE AND WRONG SIDE The wrong side of the fabric is typically a slightly faded version of the fabric print, while the print on the right side will be more pronounced. Solids can often be used interchangeably, though there may be a slight difference to the finish on the wrong side.

SCANT SEAM ALLOWANCE Used to adjust for fabric and thread bulk when a seam is pressed, a scant seam allowance takes this bulk into account by sewing just slightly under a .25 in. (.6 cm) seam allowance. With complicated blocks or quilts with many seams, a scant seam allowance is helpful to achieve perfect alignment. To sew a scant seam allowance, either move your needle slightly to the right or mark a line on your machine just inside the .25 in. (.6 cm) measurement.

SEAM ALLOWANCE Measures the distance from the line of stitching to the raw edge of the fabric piece. Many sewing machines offer a .25 in. (.6 cm) quilting foot accessory. You can also easily mark this yourself on your sewing machine using a ruler and permanent marker or tape. For quilting, a .25 in. (.6 cm) seam allowance is standard and all patterns in this book use a .25 in. (.6 cm) seam allowance (unless stated to use a scant seam allowance). A consistent seam allowance ensures seams match up when piecing the quilt top blocks together.

SELVAGE Finished edges of the fabric; often one side will have the fabric company name, designer, and fabric color or collection.

SQUARING UP The process of using a ruler and rotary cutter to ensure all edges are straight and the corners are each 90 degrees.

STITCH LENGTH Determines how much fabric is pulled through your machine between each stitch. For piecing, a stitch length of 2 mm to 2.5 mm is recommended. For quilting, a stitch length of 2.5 mm to 3.5 mm is recommended.

SUBCUT Smaller pieces that are cut from the initial WOF strips.

TEMPLATE A premade tool to cut specifically sized shapes from fabric.

TRIM SIZE The unfinished size of a block after squaring up.

WOF Width of fabric is the width of the uncut fabric measured from one selvage to the other (but not including the selvage). Most fabrics have a WOF of 42 in. to 44 in. (106.7 cm to 111.8 cm). All patterns in this book assume a 42 in. (106.7 cm) WOF.

YARDAGE Length of fabric required for making a quilt; a yard is a unit of measurement that is 36 in. (91.5 cm).

PANTOGRAPHS

The pantographs used in this book are from a variety of wonderful designers.
Here is a list of the patterns and where you can buy them.

Pillows

White Sands: "Rich Girl"
by Jess Zeigler of
Longarm League
longarmleagueshop.com

Redwood: "Wood Grain"
by Jessica Schick
urbanelementz.com

Yellowstone: "Banner"
by Haley Fetters of
Mistletoe Quilting Co.
mistletoequiltingco.com

Congaree: "Boardwalk"
by Barbara Becker
urbanelementz.com

Wall Hangings

Voyageurs: "Mid Mod
Orange Peel"
by Pro-Stitcher
prostitcher.com

Haleakala: "Driftwood"
by Jess Zeigler of
Longarm League
longarmleagueshop.com

New River Gorge: "White Space"
by Jess Zeigler of
Longarm League
longarmleagueshop.com

Indiana Dunes:
"Baptist Clamshells"
by Julie Hirt Quilts
juliehirt.com

Baby Quilts

Yosemite: "City of Fountains"
by Julie Hirt of Julie Hirt Quilts
juliehirt.com

Rocky Mountain: "Arris"
by Jessica Schick
urbanelementz.com

Everglades: "Identity"
by Karlee Porter of
Karlee Porter Designs
karleeporter.com

Zion: "Breakdown"
by Melissa Kelley of
Sew Shabby Quilting
sewshabbyquilting.com

Throw Quilts

Grand Canyon: "Curvature"
by Melissa Kelley of
Sew Shabby Quilting
sewshabbyquilting.com

Acadia: "Purl"
by Julie Hirt of Julie Hirt Quilts
juliehirt.com

Glacier Bay: "Vibrations"
by Haley Fetters of
Mistletoe Quilting Co.
mistletoequiltingco.com

Joshua Tree: "Modern Curves 1"
by Anita Shackelford
anitashackelford.net

Bed Quilts

Badlands "Fossilized"
by Jess Zeigler of
Longarm League
longarmleagueshop.com

Olympic: "Tikki Curved"
by Karlee Porter of
Karlee Porter Design
karleeporter.com

Great Smoky Mountains:
"Paradoxical"
by Jess Zeigler
of Longarm League
longarmleagueshop.com

Dry Tortugas:
"Good Vibration #1"
by Patricia E. Ritter
urbanelementz.com

ACKNOWLEDGMENTS

I would like to express my deepest gratitude to my family and friends for their support and encouragement throughout this journey.

To my husband, Kyle Peterson, for never wavering from that very first evening in our kitchen when I looked at you with determination, wine glass in hand, and told you I was turning this quilting hobby into a business. Thank you for your endless support, being my biggest cheerleader, and keeping me alive by ensuring I eat foods other than breakfast burritos and quesadillas for dinner. I am endlessly grateful to you for lending your photographic eye and capturing the stunning photographs of my finished quilts. Experiencing this life with you will forever be my greatest adventure.

To my parents, Kyle and Robin Forster, thank you for supporting my dreams and encouraging me to pursue a career that prioritizes happiness over a paycheck. To my Dad, for teaching me courage and strength to stand up for what I believe in and to not shy away from the difficult things in life. To my Mom, for teaching me kindness, humor, and unconditional love. I always have the best days with you. I wouldn't be who I am today without you both.

To my kitties, Milo, Oscar, and Rhys. Milo, your paw prints are stitched across all of my memories of making this book, from your computer supervision, photography assistance, and final product tests, I miss you every day. Oscar, your summoning powers for belly rubs encouraged many needed breaks throughout the creation of this book. Rhysie, your extra loud purrs and watching you grow from a sweet kitten to a goofy cat has been the best stress reliever and medicine for healing my broken heart.

With love and thanks to Mandy Persson, for suggesting we make quilts for our college dorms the summer after we graduated high school. You ignited a passion I didn't know was possible and started me on a creative path I never would have found otherwise. Thank you for being the best creative, enthusiastic, and adventurous friend I've ever had.

Special thanks to Emily Hoppe of So Sunny Quilts for turning these quilt tops into polished pieces of art as unique as the parks they were inspired by. Your enthusiasm and pantograph ideas breathed life into these quilts at a time when I was beyond creatively exhausted and needed a helping hand to get across the finish line.

To my technical editor, Elisabeth Myrick, thank you for being my space police and going through each of these patterns with a fine-tooth comb looking for any errors I may have missed and ensuring the instructions are clear and easy to follow.

This book would not have been possible without the collaboration of my incredible pattern testers. Thank you to Rebecca Rodgers, Emily Sadler, Kayla Dennison, Yvonne Haarbach, Emily Lanie, Amanda Eastmond, Ilana Galil, Brianne Westfield, Amanda Winchester, Lesley Weedon, Niki McCoy, Mandy Plummer, Miranda Rose, Gemma Cassells, Kate Yeater, Rachel Kaegi, Amanda Nickel, Allison Pfersich, Carrie Heyd, Sarah Lee, Sarah Bookwalter, Samantha Van de Roovaart, Miriam Lea, Mikka Tokuda-Hall, Mya Frieze, Meaghan King, Laura Boggs, Corinna Sprang, and Anja ML.

I am thankful for the expertise of Amber Elliot and her Pattern Writing Academy for teaching me how to turn my designs into written patterns. Thank you for your kindness and openness in answering all of my questions and for being an incredible guide as I navigated this book writing journey and began my small business.

I am deeply grateful to Art Gallery Fabrics for generously providing fabric for the throw and bed size quilts in this book. Forever my favorite fabric company, your enthusiasm and support of my work over the years has been invaluable.

A huge thanks to my editor, Karyn Gerhard, and my team at Insight Editions, for guiding me along this journey of writing this book. Thank you for believing in me and for fulfilling my life-long dream of becoming an author.

And finally, thanks to you, dear reader, for believing in me from my very first pattern release and coming along with me on this creative venture. My greatest hope is for you to find inspiration in these projects and for you to set out on your own adventure.

weldon**owen**

an imprint of Insight Editions
P.O. Box 3088
San Rafael, CA 94912
www.weldonowen.com

CEO Raoul Goff
SVP, Group Publisher Jeff McLaughlin
VP Publisher Roger Shaw
Senior Editor Karyn Gerhard
Editorial Assistant Jon Ellis
VP Creative Chrissy Kwasnik
Art Director and Designer Allister Fein
VP Manufacturing Alix Nicholaeff
Sr Production Manager Joshua Smith
Strategic Production Planner
Lina s Palma-Temena

Weldon Owen would also like to thank
Carla Kipen and Karen Levy for their
work on this project.

ISBN: 979-8-88674-171-1

Manufactured in China by Insight Editions
10 9 8 7 6 5 4 3 2 1

ROOTS of PEACE   REPLANTED PAPER

Insight Editions, in association with Roots of
Peace, will plant two trees for each tree used in
the manufacturing of this book. Roots of Peace
is an internationally renowned humanitarian
organization dedicated to eradicating land
mines worldwide and converting war-torn
lands into productive farms and wildlife
habitats. Roots of Peace will plant two million
fruit and nut trees in Afghanistan and provide
farmers there with the skills and support
necessary for sustainable land use.

ABOUT THE AUTHOR

An avid creator and outdoor enthusiast, Stephanie Forster has been quilting for more than fifteen years. Her quilt patterns are often inspired by elements found in nature.

Originally from Bismarck, North Dakota, Stephanie grew up camping with her family and spending time at their lake cabin in the summers. An artist from a young age, she has always enjoyed bringing the natural world indoors through drawing and painting.

As a licensed mental health counselor and art therapist, she works with children and families in crisis. You can find her at www.bookendsquilting.com and at Bookends Quilting on Instagram and TikTok, where she shares current projects and books she's reading. She lives in Seattle, Washington, with her husband and cats, and enjoys spending time outdoors biking, hiking, running, and snowboarding.